FAITH, HOPE, AND CLARITY
How to Know God's Will

GARY ZIMAK

servant

AN IMPRINT OF
FRANCISCAN MEDIA
Cincinnati, Ohio

Scripture passages have been taken from the *Revised Standard Version*, Catholic edition. Copyright 1946, 1952, 1971 by the Division of Christian Education of the National Council of Churches of Christ in the USA. Used by permission. All rights reserved. Quotes are taken from the English translation of the *Catechism of the Catholic Church* for the United States of America (indicated as *CCC*), 2nd ed. Copyright 1997 by United States Catholic Conference—Libreria Editrice Vaticana.

Cover design by Candle Light Studio
Book design by Mark Sullivan

ISBN 978-1-61636-884-5

Published by Servant Books, an imprint of Franciscan Media.
28 W. Liberty St.
Cincinnati, OH 45202
www.FranciscanMedia.org

Printed in the United States of America.
Printed on acid-free paper.
15 16 17 18 19 5 4 3 2 1

DEDICATION

To my wife, Eileen:
Thank you for your unconditional love and support.
You are a great blessing, and I love you!

To my daughters, Mary and Elizabeth:
Thank you for loving me and for being so enthusiastic about my work.
Always remember to stay close to Jesus and Mary.
They love you greatly, and so do I!

To Jesus Christ:
Thank you for being so patient with me.
Please help me to continually surrender to your will.
I love you, Lord!

To my Blessed Mother Mary:
Thank you for everything. I love you!

Contents

FOREWORD
Donna-Marie Cooper O'Boyle

TRYING TO FIGURE OUT HOW WE ARE TO LIVE OUR LIFE SO WE CAN please God can be a very daunting endeavor. Some seasons of our life are laden with utter busyness, and during these times, we might not have much of a care regarding what we *should* be doing because we are just so occupied with checking off everything on our "to-do" lists. Or perhaps we might be dealing with some very serious issues that require all our energy and attention, and there's no question—focusing all our energy on these issues is exactly what we should be doing.

But there certainly are the times in between when deep down, in the depths of our heart, we know without a doubt that we are being beckoned to make a decision—one way or the other—this direction or that—and we need to pause and ponder, and perhaps most especially, we need to pray. *What does God want of me? What should I do?*

I remember well praying long and hard to discern what God wanted me to do at a particular time in my life. I had recently met Blessed Mother Teresa of Calcutta, and I was very drawn to her charism of serving the poorest of the poor. I desired to become a Lay Missionary of Charity, which is the lay branch of Mother Teresa's religious order.

At the time, though, I was already a member of the Third Order of St. Dominic. Because I couldn't be a member of both orders—it wasn't allowed—I began to pray about the direction I sensed God was calling me.

St. Dominic possessed an intense love for Christ and the Church and therefore was passionately zealous for the conversion of souls. The charisms, or pillars, of the Order of St. Dominic are prayer, study, community life, and apostolate. Each of them is very essential to Dominican spirituality because each forms the Dominican for more effective preaching of Christ to the world. The call for a Dominican to preach is exercised in the apostolic life. The benefits of one's prayer, study, and community life are steeped through one's preaching (apostolate).

This, of course, is very good indeed, and I had greatly benefited by being a lay member of the order, but now it seemed that every part of me deeply yearned to join Mother Teresa's order as a layperson. Mother Teresa also dearly loved Christ and his Church; she also was intensely zealous about saving souls. I loved the idea of growing in holiness in that walk of life—following the example and wisdom of Mother Teresa, a modern-day saint, one who was with us now. I appreciated the distinctive calling in the lay Missionaries of Charity regarding the sanctification of the family. It truly spoke to me, for I was immersed in the care of my family.

The Missionaries of Charity sisters had asked me if I would like to join the Lay Missionaries of Charity, and they even encouraged me to start a branch of it in my area of Connecticut. I met with a member of the Lay Missionaries of Charity to learn more.

I continued to pray about it all, and I earnestly hoped to be able to discern what God wanted me to do before too long. After about three months of praying, I decided that I should join Mother Teresa's order as a lay member. In order to do so, I would need to consult with the hierarchy of the Dominican order in charge of the Third Order. I discussed my inclinations, and before long, I was given permission to leave the Dominicans to join the Lay Missionaries of Charity.

I went ahead and started the branch of the Lay Missionaries of Charity at my parish, and it began to attract members immediately.

I still feel close to the Dominican order, and I feel that being a member of the Third Order was an important bridge that led to me joining Mother Teresa's order. Both of these lay orders are an excellent means to grow in holiness while living as laity in the world.

Discernment, however, is not reserved for those attempting to figure out a call to religious life or a lay order. Everyone is involved in discernment in a myriad of ways, even at times when one is simply immersed in one's normal daily activities. Even so, at times, making an effort to know what God wants you to do can be downright intimidating and perplexing. But don't give up!

Author Gary Zimak admits that he has wrestled with the question "What does God want me to do?" throughout his life. Facing uncertainty and the unknown can feel pretty scary at times. Not knowing what to do in the big, important things as well as in the smaller, everyday details can challenge us to the core and even rob us of our peace.

I really love that Gary Zimak has put his fingers to the keys and expressed his wisdom and experience from the trenches of life to help others discover God's will in their own lives. I believe that discernment is a very important course of action. Thankfully, in this book, Gary offers the nuts and bolts of the discerning process in a very conversational and encouraging way. You'll feel as though Gary is your personal spiritual advisor, taking you through the steps one at a time, all the while lovingly cheering you on to continue forward on your journey.

Gary instructs us in this book, "Don't try to become holy all by yourself. Always ask the Lord for help. He'll never let you down." He knows without a doubt that working on one's relationship with our Lord is paramount. Our primary goal is getting closer to Jesus and living our faith daily. They naturally go hand in hand.

I'll let you in on something personal about Gary. Whenever (and I mean whenever!) Gary and I get together at conferences and events, or even when we speak on the phone or by videoconferencing, we end up spending a good deal of time laughing together. Gary is full of Christian joy, and it's contagious. Christian joy is something Mother Teresa really loved.

While I know the subject of this book is of a serious nature and not a laughing matter, I suspect that you will come away from this book knowing Gary more personally because he openly shares his heart so joyfully with his readers, striving to bring them closer to heaven.

You are in for a treat, as well as possibly a life-transforming experience!

INTRODUCTION

God has created me to do Him some definite service; he has committed some work to me which He has not committed to another.[1]

—Cardinal John Henry Newman

"WHAT DOES GOD WANT ME TO DO?" THAT'S A QUESTION THAT I'VE wrestled with many times over the course of my life. One occurrence, however, is particularly etched in my memory.

In fall 2009, I was sitting on a bench in Manasquan, New Jersey, listening to my iPod. I had taken a vacation day from my job as a computer programmer and was enjoying the sun while my wife and daughters shopped at the outlet stores. Allowing my iPod to randomly pick the songs, I was enjoying back-to-back selections by John Michael Talbot: "Here I Am, Lord" and "Be Not Afraid."

Listening to these songs, I got the crazy idea that God might want me to work full-time as a Catholic lay evangelist. Ignoring the feeling of peace that I immediately experienced, I dismissed the idea and reminded myself that "normal" people don't think this way. After all, I was the sole provider for my family, and I would be foolish to give up a six-figure income for the insecurity of such a job. Although I brushed off that silly thought that day, I would end up considering it again and again.

How often do you think about what God wants you to do in your life? Not only with the big things but also with the everyday decisions? Each day, the Lord gives us many chances to respond to his call. We deal with people and are placed in situations that allow us to say yes to God.

If you're like me, you've probably prayed the Lord's Prayer thousands of times. You have spoken the words "Thy will be done" at least that many times. But even though we express that sentiment, do we really mean it? And if we mean it, how do we know what God wants us to do?

For many of us, trying to figure out what God wants us to do can be very intimidating. If you feel that way, relax! The Lord doesn't want us to be in the dark. If he wants us to do something, he will let us know. Unfortunately, we often fail to listen, don't know how to listen, or can't believe what he is asking us to do.

Although it may take time, determining what God wants us to do isn't impossible or even extremely difficult. It simply takes a combination of common sense, willingness to seek him out, and desire to listen to what he is saying. How do I know?

After years of being a lukewarm Catholic, a health scare in 2004 caused me to embrace my faith in a big way. As time progressed, my love for Christ and his Church grew stronger, which gradually increased my desire to live according to God's plan instead of my plan. As my commitment to Christ grew, opportunities began to come my way for sharing my faith personally and through various forms of media. And as I took those opportunities, I regularly felt the peace that comes from doing the will of God.

After the incident on the New Jersey park bench, I began to wonder whether God might be calling me to make a change in my occupation. A time of discernment followed, involving much prayer, soul searching, conversations with my wife and Catholic colleagues, and regular sessions with my spiritual director. While I was strongly drawn to full-time Christian work, I keenly felt the responsibility of providing adequately for my family's needs.

And then it happened: For the first time in my thirty-year career, I was laid off from my job. My reaction was a combination of dread and relief. I was nervous but peaceful.

Through all the ensuing twists and turns that leaving my IT career entailed, God's providence never wavered. Losing my job opened the door for me to follow what I sensed was God's leading in my life—a new career as a full-time Christian speaker and writer. It has been almost four years now, and along the way, I have discovered a great deal about discerning the Lord's will. I'm anxious to share this knowledge with others.

Are you trying to live according to God's will? Do you feel that he's calling you to do something, but you have doubts? I wrote this book for you!

Whether you're facing a major decision (a religious vocation, career change, marriage) or a relatively minor one (volunteering at your parish, buying a new car, deciding whether to take a vacation with your family), I'll share a simple approach to guide you along the way. Each chapter focuses on a different aspect of discernment and includes reflection questions designed to help you adapt the material to your own situation.

If the Lord wants you to do something, he will let you know. God has a plan for you. Let's look at some ways to hear his voice more clearly and put his plan into action!

Make me to know thy ways, O Lord;
teach me thy paths. (Psalm 25:4)

CHAPTER ONE

Decisions, Decisions

Every day, you and I are faced with many decisions. Sometimes these choices are so subconscious that we don't even realize that we are making decisions. What time should I wake up? What clothes should I wear? What should I have for breakfast? What radio program should I listen to on the way to work? What is the first thing I should do when I get to the office? What should I have for lunch?

Some decisions are important, and some are trivial, but we have to respond in some way. Whether we think about it or not, making choices is a regular part of our daily routine.

OK, get ready, because I'm about to ask you a tough question. How often do you consult with God before making decisions? Good question, right? If you think about it long enough, you'll probably realize that you make many decisions without asking the Lord how you should act.

Can I Get Some Help Here?

If you're like me, you tend to seek help when you're dealing with an unfamiliar situation. For example, when buying a new car, I do some research on the Internet and then talk to my friends. "I'm thinking of buying a new car. Is this a good model? What dealership should I visit?"

This is a very wise thing to do when venturing into uncharted waters. Purchasing a house, hiring someone to do home repairs, and choosing a new doctor are among the situations in which we might seek others' advice and opinions. Furthermore, we're going to choose someone who is familiar with the area in question. Asking a plumber for the best way to change an electrical outlet is probably not a good idea. (I don't know a lot about home repairs, but even I know that water and electricity don't mix!)

The point is that seeking the advice of an expert is almost second nature to us when we are faced with unfamiliar choices. We do it because we want to make informed decisions; we want to make good choices.

Aside from the practical reasons, consulting with another person can often be a matter of courtesy. For example, I wouldn't make a major purchase without checking with my wife. Why? Because it's the right thing to do in the relationship. Suppose you need some information at work. Before sending an e-mail or setting up an appointment with the top executive, it would be appropriate to consult your immediate supervisor, even though you're pretty sure the CEO of the company has what you need. In the military, this is referred to as respecting the chain of command. Not only is this a good business practice, but it's the right thing to do in terms of your relationship with your supervisor.

Whether it's because he knows more than we do or simply out of courtesy, the Lord should be an important part of our decision-making process. St. Ignatius of Loyola teaches that we should base all of our choices on what brings glory to God and pleases him, not on what feels good to us.

Obviously, it doesn't matter to God what kind of ice cream we eat or what condiments we put on our hamburgers. But he certainly cares about many of our decisions. Too often, we forget this, which can lead to a habit of making decisions without turning to God at all. So, what exactly is an "important" decision?

I'm sure we can agree on some obvious ones: entering the religious life, choosing a college, relocating for a new job, getting married, having another child. What about moving to a bigger house or taking a vacation? These might seem "kind of" important and may or may not be brought to the Lord, depending on the individual.

Finally, what do you think about buying a cup of coffee every day on the way to work, going out to eat, making a phone call, or watching your favorite program on television? Before you classify these as "not important" decisions, consider a few things. Your daily coffee expenditure could easily amount to five hundred dollars per year, which would make a very generous charitable contribution. Making a phone call to a lonely friend or relative could be a nice way of practicing charity. Choosing to turn off the television and speak with God in prayer would be a very productive use of your time.

Surprising, isn't it? When we stop to think about it, many "trivial" decisions might not be so trivial after all.

Are you beginning to see how God may be interested in some of your routine decisions? And if that's the case, doesn't it follow that you should probably consult him about these decisions?

If this makes you uncomfortable, let me assure you that it's not as bad as it sounds. As we've already established, some decisions are more important than others, and we could easily drive ourselves crazy by overthinking the less important ones. You don't need to check in with God every time you buy a pack of gum. Let's put things in perspective.

How can we tell if a decision is truly important? How do we know if we should pray before acting? It really boils down to one simple question, one we should get used to asking ourselves frequently: "Does this decision affect my relationship with God?"

If the answer is "yes," then we absolutely should consult with him as part of our decision making process. Now, before you begin to panic because you have been ignoring God for most of your life or feel that this method will never work for you, let's take a minute to discuss a few things. I think you'll find that this concept is very easy to put into practice.

THE MOST IMPORTANT RELATIONSHIP

When I mentioned not wanting to make a major purchase without consulting my wife, the main reason was because we are in a relationship, and I love her. I never want to do something that will hurt her in any way. After all, love is about dying to self and putting the needs of others before your own.

Fortunately, I have been blessed with a wonderful wife who feels the same way I do. Therefore, we always talk before making any important decisions. What's an important decision? You got it, anything that affects our relationship.

Is it always easy to figure out what's important? Not always. In any relationship, what's important to one person may not be important to the other person. Often, something seemingly trivial to me can actually mean a great deal to my wife. This signals the need for communication and for working on our relationship.

From the time she was a young girl, my wife was very close to her mother. When we first got married, Eileen would sometimes consult her mother for help before she came to me. She wasn't trying to exclude me, but she was simply used to relying on her mother's advice when making a decision. In reality, however, I felt excluded. I felt that she should discuss certain matters with me first.

When I told Eileen how I felt, she was surprised. She had never thought that this would bother me. Realizing that I was hurt by this practice, however, she started making it a point to discuss important matters with me first.

Being in a relationship doesn't give us the power to read minds, and therefore, communication is essential. In addition, good relationships don't just happen; they require work. If both parties are willing to work, the relationship is going to flourish.

Our relationship with the Lord is no different. We know that he loves us, and we can rest assured that he is doing his part to help the relationship grow. How much does God love us? "For God so loved the world that he gave his only Son, that whoever believes in him should not perish but have eternal life" (John 3:16).

Our Father's love can be summed up in one word: Jesus! Throughout history, God has reached out to his people with unconditional love. This love reached its climax when he sent his Son to become our redeemer. Through Jesus, it's possible to have a personal relationship with Almighty God. Not only is it possible for us to have this relationship, but the Lord desires it. Personal relationship with him is an awesome privilege, and we should welcome it. "Behold, I stand at the door and knock; if any one hears my voice and opens the door, I will come in to him and eat with him, and he with me" (Revelation 3:20).

The fact that you're reading a book about discovering God's will probably indicates that you would like to take him up on his generous offer. Now, if you're questioning just how well you and the Lord know one another, please don't worry. I'll discuss this in depth and offer suggestions for improving the relationship in the next chapter. For now, take comfort in the fact that God loves you and wants to have a deep personal relationship with you!

Put aside all doubts about the current state of your relationship and make a formal expression of your desire to get to know him better.

You can use your own words or simply say, "Lord, I want to enter a deeper relationship with you, and I desire to do your will." Don't worry about how you feel or what you fear; don't be concerned about your ability to follow through. Just say it and let it come from the heart. If you don't have the desire, ask for it! Once you express that desire, God will respond. If you tell him that you want to get to know him better, I guarantee that he will help you.

God Is Our Helper

We sometimes try to do everything on our own, forgetting that the Lord wants to help us. Let's never be afraid to admit that we're weak and can't do things on our own. St. Paul gives us a great example: "On my own behalf I will not boast, except of my weaknesses" (2 Corinthians 12:5).

Paul understood how much he needed God's help:

> I will all the more gladly boast of my weaknesses, that the power of Christ may rest upon me. For the sake of Christ, then, I am content with weaknesses, insults, hardships, persecutions, and calamities; for when I am weak, then I am strong. (2 Corinthians 12:9–10)

Don't try to become holy all by yourself. Always ask the Lord for help. He'll never let you down.

Rather than trying to compile a detailed list of the decisions that the Lord cares about, here's what I recommend: Make a commitment to work on your relationship with Jesus on a daily basis. Speak with him in prayer, receive the sacraments, and let him speak to you through sacred Scripture. Make it a point to express daily your desire for a deeper relationship with the Lord. Devote time to working on your relationship with him every day.

As in the relationship between my wife and me, as you grow closer to Jesus, you will better understand what he wants you to do. You will know when a choice will offend him. You will understand what makes him happy and what makes him sad. Eventually, you'll be able to make choices that please the Lord without giving it too much thought. Why? Because you know him personally. It will become as natural as buying your spouse a birthday present.

Are you getting excited? Do you feel that it's really possible to have a close personal relationship with Jesus? Are you starting to believe that you'll be able to make decisions that conform to his will? Good, because it is not only possible but very achievable.

I have just scratched the surface of how and why we should involve God in our decision making. He loves us, and he wants to be intimately involved in our lives, but he won't force us to include him. In the following chapters, I'll explore how to let him guide us. And remember, it's going to be much easier than you think!

Key Points
1. We make many decisions, big and small, every day.
2. Many of our decisions can impact our relationship with the Lord.
3. God wants to have a relationship with us and become involved in our lives.
4. God will not force himself on us. He knocks but waits for us to open the door.
5. The more we get to know Jesus personally, the more we'll learn what makes him happy.

Reflection Questions
1. How often do you speak with the Lord during the day?
2. Think about all of the decisions you've made in the last twenty-four hours. How many times did you consult God before acting?

3. Do you have a sincere desire to please God, even if it causes you discomfort?

4. How has God revealed himself to you in the last day?

5. Do you ever think about how much God loves you? After doing so, how do you express your love for him?

CHAPTER TWO

Getting to Know the Lord

I'VE ALWAYS HAD A FASCINATION WITH HISTORY. WHEN I WAS YOUNG, I thoroughly enjoyed reading about the presidents of the United States. Out of all the presidents, I was particularly interested in Theodore Roosevelt. In an effort to get to know more about him, I sought out pictures, books, and material on his life. As a result, I was able to learn a great deal about him.

Despite getting to know much *about* President Theodore Roosevelt, however, I never was able to *know* him as a person. I couldn't ask him questions or be in his presence because he died many years before I was born. Although I knew many facts about him, it was not possible for me to have a personal relationship with Theodore Roosevelt.

Unfortunately, many of us treat Jesus in the same way. We know that he lived two thousand years ago, we know some facts about his life, we are even familiar with things that he said—and it ends there. We make the mistake of treating him just like any other historical figure. We do not even consider the fact that it is possible to have a personal relationship with him.

Thinking that we can't have a personal relationship with Jesus could not be further from the truth. Furthermore, if we want to be able to make decisions in accordance with Jesus's will, we absolutely must get to know him personally. The good news is that, even though the idea can seem intimidating, we can all have a relationship with Jesus by following a few simple steps.

For most of my life, my relationship with Jesus was not a good one. Even though I went to Mass every week, I viewed him as a cross between a historical figure and an "imaginary friend." I accepted the fact that he did exist, was crucified, rose from the dead, and ascended into heaven. I was even able to quote some of the things he said. I even prayed on occasion, or at least went through the motions.

I did know where to find Jesus when I needed a favor. Having heard stories of answered prayers and even miracles in the lives of others, I thought that I should pray when I needed something. After all, Jesus said that if we ask, we'll receive. Praying for my needs was a matter of covering all the bases.

Fortunately, although it took me many years, I came to discover that it is possible to have a personal relationship with Jesus. What's even more amazing is that he wants this relationship more than I do! "Behold, I stand at the door and knock; if any one hears my voice and opens the door, I will come in to him and eat with him, and he with me" (Revelation 3:20).

Even though Jesus wants to become intimate friends with us, isn't it incredible that he won't force us to respond to his offer? Despite the fact that friendship with Christ is the answer to achieving peace, discovering his will for our lives, and getting to heaven, he won't *force us* to become his friends. If we choose to ignore him, as I did for many years, he will let us.

Jesus will stand at our door, knock, and wait patiently for us to invite him into our lives. Once we open the door and allow him to come inside, great things will happen. In the remainder of this chapter, we'll explore some practical ways for getting to know Jesus personally.

PRAY!

What exactly is a personal relationship? Simply put, it's a relationship between two individuals. In order for this relationship to develop and grow, two-way communication is needed. The fact that you're reading my words doesn't necessarily mean that you and I have a personal relationship. In order for a relationship to exist, both parties need to express themselves to one another.

A relationship with Jesus works in exactly the same way. While your relationship with the Lord should also involve responding to his unconditional love by loving him in return, the basic thing needed is communication. If you speak to Jesus and he speaks to you, a personal relationship does exist. While your relationship shouldn't end there, this two-way communication provides a foundation on which to build.

Now that we're aware that Jesus is knocking on our door, how do we go about opening the door and letting him in? It all begins with prayer. If we want to know the Lord, we absolutely and positively must speak to him in prayer. Furthermore, if we are going to have a *good* personal relationship with Jesus, we must pray every day. If you only remember one thing from this chapter, this is it! *It is impossible to have a good personal relationship with Jesus without daily prayer.*

No matter how much we desire to do God's will, we will encounter days when we don't want to pray. While there is nothing wrong with having those feelings (they are neither right nor wrong), there is something wrong with letting our emotions drive our spiritual life. In order to develop and maintain a good personal relationship with Christ, daily prayer is a necessity.

Even after making a commitment to spend time in prayer each day, there are many questions that can arise. What's the best way to pray? When should I pray? How many times do I have to pray each day?

While there can be many answers to such questions, I would like to share what works for me. I have wrestled with these questions over the years and have found that some methods are more effective than others.

The most important thing to remember is that prayer should be a conversation with the Lord. We should never lose sight of the fact that, when we pray, he is listening. This intimate conversation can exist whether we use formal prayers or our own words. I have found that a combination of formal and spontaneous prayer works best for me.

People sometimes refrain from formal prayers (such as the Our Father or Hail Mary) because they feel that such prayers don't allow for a meaningful conversation. I strongly disagree. When one of his disciples asked Jesus, "Lord, teach us to pray," he responded by reciting the Lord's Prayer (see Luke 11:1–4). How could a prayer composed by Jesus be ineffective or meaningless?

I pray the Our Father several times throughout the day and find that it helps me overcome one of my big weaknesses. When I pray, I have a tendency to focus on myself. My natural instinct is to concentrate mainly on *my* needs and wants. And while the Lord certainly wants us to present him with our needs and desires, it is more important to concentrate on his desires.

As soon as I pray the opening words, "Our Father," I'm reminded that he's not just *my* Father. I'm also praying on behalf of his other children around the world. Then, turning my attention to "hallowed be thy name," I offer prayers of praise to Almighty God. I then proceed to pray that his will be done on earth, just as it is in heaven. It's only then that I ask him to "give us this day our daily bread."

Again, the words *us* and *our* imply that this prayer is bigger than me. I'm praying that the starving children in the world can have food to eat before the day is over. I'm praying that the financially strapped single mother can pay her rent. And I'm praying that the Lord will continue to nourish us with his very Body, Blood, soul, and divinity in the Eucharist.

I conclude my prayer by asking that we all be kept free from temptation and be delivered from evil. What an awesome privilege! I am asking the Lord to grant everyone in the world the grace that they need to get to heaven.

There is no doubt that we can use formal prayers incorrectly. Perhaps we simply recite the words rather than praying from the heart. Yet, the benefits of the Our Father and other formal prayers far outweigh that risk.

In addition to formal prayers, I also speak to the Lord using my own words. What do I say? Anything that comes to mind! I tell him that I love him, I thank him for the many blessings in my life, I ask for the strength to deal with difficult situations, and I share my thoughts with him. I have to admit that this was difficult for me at first, but it gets easier each day.

If the idea of speaking to Jesus in a conversational way seems foreign to you, I recommend that you start slowly and ask him to help you. Because we depend so much on our senses, most of us find it difficult to communicate with a person we cannot see. That's perfectly understandable, but this can change over time. What you need to remember is that you are not conversing with an imaginary friend when you are speaking to the Lord. You are having a conversation with someone who is very real.

Jesus wants to communicate with you as well. Even though it may not feel like it, speaking with the Lord always involves reciprocation on his part. He may speak mysteriously, he may speak in silence, or sometimes you may even be able to audibly hear his words. However he speaks, you can rest assured that Jesus will not ignore you.

Over time, you will feel Jesus's presence more and more in your prayer. In the meantime, make sure that you speak to Jesus throughout the day.

If you don't feel like it or don't feel it's doing any good, do it anyway. Day by day, your friendship will grow, and you'll find yourself looking forward to chatting with the Lord about anything and everything.

TIME FOR GOD

When should I pray? While it's a great idea to converse with the Lord throughout the day, there are two times that you should definitely pray: *as soon as you wake up* and *before you go to sleep*.

For many years, I woke up and never said anything to the Lord. I grumbled about the weather, complained about my boring job, thought about the weekend, but never thanked the Lord for giving me another day to know, love, and serve him. Immediately upon arising, I now say, "Lord, thank you for giving me another day. I surrender to your will. Please grant me the grace to hear and obey you today."

While it only takes a few seconds, that simple prayer sets the tone for the entire day. In those few words, I express my gratitude to the Lord, submit to his will in all things (a great expression of love for him), and ask for the grace to act as he would act in all situations that I encounter throughout the day. Each new day is a gift from the Lord. Beginning with prayer keeps the distractions of daily life at bay, so that we do not lose sight of God's plan.

St. Paul instructs us to "pray constantly" (1 Thessalonians 5:17), but how is that possible? What about our other duties? The idea of praying constantly is a challenging one that definitely warrants further explanation.

Believe it or not, this instruction is actually quite doable. St. Paul is encouraging us to dedicate all of our daily activities to the Lord. By doing that, our entire day becomes a continuous prayer. Simple, isn't it?

One of the most effective ways to express this desire is by reciting the Morning Offering. There are several variations of this prayer (you can even use your own words), but here is one of the most popular forms:

O Jesus, through the Immaculate Heart of Mary,
I offer you my prayers, works, joys, and sufferings of this day,
for all the intentions of your Sacred Heart,
in union with the Holy Sacrifice of the Mass throughout the
world,
in reparation for my sins,
for the intentions of all my relatives and friends,
and in particular for the intentions of the Holy Father.
Amen.

The other time that it's important to pray is just before you go to sleep. This is a great time to do a brief examination of conscience. It's a simple process, and it is essential when you're trying to do God's will.

An examination of conscience involves a few minutes reviewing the day (ask the Holy Spirit to help you), calling to mind each time that your actions pleased or displeased God. If you sinned, or acted in a way that might have offended the Lord, simply tell him that you're sorry, ask for the grace to do better tomorrow, and if the sin was serious or mortal, resolve to go to confession as soon as possible. In those cases where you behaved in a way that pleased the Lord, thank him for the grace that allowed you to do the right thing and ask for his continued help.

In addition, one of my favorite nighttime reflections—I often read it just before lying down and think about it as I'm falling asleep—is this passage from Psalm 63. It's a great reminder of the many blessings God provides and of our dependence on him:

My soul is feasted as with marrow and fat,
    and my mouth praises thee with joyful lips,
when I think of thee upon my bed,
    and meditate on thee in the watches of the night;

for thou hast been my help,
    and in the shadow of thy wings I sing for joy.
My soul clings to you;
    thy right hand upholds me. (Psalm 63:5–8)

An active prayer life is essential to knowing and loving Jesus. But it's not the only component. Let's look at some other methods of getting to know the Lord.

READ THE BIBLE

One of the biggest mistakes we can make is to treat the Bible as "just another book." While there's no doubt that Jesus was a historical figure, there's a big difference between reading the Gospels and reading about Abraham Lincoln. When we open the Bible, we have an encounter with the Lord, and he speaks to us. That's a claim no other book in the world can make.

If we want to know Jesus better, reading the Bible is indispensable. And although God is the author of the entire Bible (see *CCC* 105; *Dei Verbum*, 11), the Gospels hold a place of prominence and "are the heart of all the Scriptures 'because they are our principal source for the life and teaching of the Incarnate Word, our Savior'" (*CCC* 125, quoting *Dei Verbum*, 18). Reading the Gospels was so important to St. Ignatius of Loyola that he made it a mandatory part of his Spiritual Exercises.

As with prayer, the appropriate amount of time spent on Bible reading varies by individual. If you're not used to reading Scripture, I recommend that you start slowly. Pledging to faithfully read God's written Word for five minutes each day is much more realistic than pledging to read for one or two hours. I am always amazed at how the Lord can speak to me in a few words or a single Bible verse. His voice is powerful, and he can pack a lot into one or two sentences.

While you can certainly start with the Gospel of Matthew and work your way through Mark, Luke, and John, another good way to read the Bible is to follow the daily Mass readings. With the aid of a missal, a magazine such as *Magnificat* or *The Word Among Us*, or online readings (www.usccb.org is a good source), you can let the Church guide you through the Bible.

As we meet the Lord in the pages of Scripture, we get to know him better. We begin to understand how he thinks and how he would like us to behave in any given situation. And unlike most books we read, we can ask the author questions about the material!

As I read about the storm at sea (see Matthew 8:23–27), I hear the Lord admonishing me for my weak faith and assuring me that he can calm all of the storms in my life. I can then reflect on my problems and ask for his assistance.

The encounter between Mary and Gabriel (see Luke 1:26–38) gives me the opportunity to ask the Lord how I can best serve him. It also reminds me to trust in his providence, especially when I'm faced with uncertainty. I can ask for the grace to trust him more.

Conversing with Jesus through Scripture will strengthen our relationship and help us to know him in an intimate way. "All Scripture is inspired by God and profitable for teaching, for reproof, for correction, and for training in righteousness, that the man of God may be complete, equipped for every good work" (2 Timothy 3:16–17).

THE SACRAMENTS

I could easily devote an entire book to the power of the sacraments. What's important for us to understand here is that we meet Jesus when we receive the sacraments. As with any relationship, the best way to get to know someone is to spend time in his or her presence. Therefore, receiving the sacraments is a great way to get to know and love Jesus.

Since a close personal relationship with the Lord is necessary if we expect to follow his will, we should make it a point to receive the sacraments as often as possible. When I started to receive Holy Communion daily and confession biweekly, I got to know Christ better than I had thought possible.

The Church teaches that Jesus "acts through the sacraments" (*CCC* 1076). Furthermore, "[b]y his power he is present in the sacraments so that when anybody baptizes, it is really Christ himself who baptizes" (*CCC* 1088, quoting *Sacrosanctum Concilium*, 7). The Eucharist is recognized as the "Sacrament of sacraments" (*CCC* 1211). There is no better way to know Christ than to receive him frequently in Holy Communion. When you combine that with daily prayer and Bible reading, you will get to know Jesus *very* well!

Eucharistic adoration is a powerful way to spend time with the Lord, who patiently waits for us to visit him. When I began visiting the adoration chapel, I didn't know what to say, and I kept looking at my watch. Over time, I grew to love being in the Lord's presence, and now I am sad when I have to leave him. All of my books were at least partially written in the presence of the Lord at my local adoration chapel.

If you're not accustomed to spending time before the Blessed Sacrament, I recommend that you visit an adoration chapel or church today and spend fifteen minutes with the Lord. You can share your thoughts with him or simply rest quietly in his presence. It might take several times, but you will eventually begin to look forward to visiting with the best friend any of us could ever have.

Jesus is knocking on your door and wants to be your friend. Will you let him in?

KEY POINTS:
1. We get to know Jesus through prayer, Bible reading, and the reception of the sacraments.

2. Prayer is a conversation with the Lord.

3. When we read the Bible, God speaks to us.

4. Jesus acts through the sacraments.

5. The Eucharist is the "Sacrament of sacraments" and should be received as often as possible.

REFLECTION QUESTIONS:

1. Have you conversed with the Lord today? What did you discuss?

2. Do you make a conscious effort to hear Jesus speaking? Is it difficult?

3. Read the Gospel for today's Mass. What is God saying to you through this passage?

4. Would you like to receive Holy Communion more often? How can you make that happen?

5. Do you really know Jesus? How can you know him better?

CHAPTER THREE

Use Your Head

THE WORD *DISCERNMENT* CAN BE A LITTLE OVERWHELMING. WE
sometimes think of it as a long and drawn out process, and we often
tie it to vocation decisions. But that's only one aspect of discernment.

While discernment needs to be part of the game plan for those who
feel called to the religious life, it's also essential for the members of
the laity who are striving to follow God's will. And to take it a step
further, it's not just applicable to long-term vocational decisions such as
marriage and choice of career but also to our daily lives. As we discussed
in the first chapter, if we're in a relationship with the Lord, he should be
involved in all our decisions.

For the purposes of this book, *discernment* refers to our desire to
figure out what God wants us to do. Now, here's the good news: Much
of the discernment process boils down to common sense.

Wait a minute! What happened to the part about involving God in
our decision making?

By using common sense, that's exactly what we're doing.

GOD GAVE ME A BRAIN

The Lord has given us human beings the ability to reason. We have an
intellect and are able to use our reasoning skills to arrive at logical decisions. As long as our conclusions don't conflict with any of the Lord's
teachings, he absolutely expects us to use our intelligence.

In the parable of the wise and foolish maidens, Jesus emphasizes the need for us to use our intelligence in making decisions:

> Then the kingdom of heaven shall be compared to ten maidens who took their lamps and went to meet the bridegroom. Five of them were foolish, and five were wise. For when the foolish took their lamps, they took no oil with them; but the wise took flasks of oil with their lamps. (Matthew 25:1–4)

In this well-known parable, Jesus reminds us of the fact that our time on earth is limited. We don't know when our time will be up and we'll be facing our judgment. He's telling us to imitate the wise maidens, who prepared for a long wait and brought extra oil for their lamps.

The foolish maidens, on the other hand, were unprepared and were unable to escort the bridegroom to the wedding feast because their lamps had run out of oil. Could they have used their intellect to reason that there was a possibility that their lamps would run out of oil before the bridegroom arrived? Absolutely. They obviously didn't think it through. A little common sense goes a long way when it comes to determining what God wants us to do.

With the help of our intellect, under the guidance of the Lord and his Church, we can often make God-inspired choices with little effort and in a relatively short period of time. For one thing, we can rule out potential choices that aren't practical or that conflict with our state in life. In other words, some options can immediately be ruled out because they don't make sense.

For example, let's look at that big question for unmarried men and women who are sincerely trying to follow God's will: "Am I being called to the priesthood or the religious life?" As someone who didn't get married until the age of thirty-five, I wrestled with this exact question.

When I was in my early thirties, I became involved with a young adult group in my parish. I hate to admit it, but spiritual growth wasn't my top priority. Rather, I was mainly there to meet a "nice, Catholic girl." But it wasn't happening.

For several months, I faithfully attended the biweekly meetings. We prayed the rosary, participated in adoration of the Blessed Sacrament, and listened to an assortment of excellent Catholic speakers. As he so often does, the Lord ended up touching my heart in an unexpected way, and I began to grow closer and closer to him.

While that was a good thing, I still felt sad about not meeting a potential wife. Although I didn't date much (I was way too shy!), I felt called to the vocation of marriage and thought that I would make a good husband and father. But since it wasn't happening, I felt compelled to address the question that I absolutely did not want to address: "Is God calling me to become a priest?"

Why was this such a difficult question for me to address? I had no desire to be a priest, never once felt called to be a priest, and literally would cringe at the idea. Facing those feelings, I thought that maybe I was being selfish. So I prayed about it. In all honesty, the prayer went something like, "Lord, please don't make me have to become a priest!"

One day, I picked up a brochure designed to help you determine if you have a religious vocation. With sweaty hands and a racing heart-beat (I'm not kidding), I opened the brochure, read one line, and felt a great sense of peace. It was a statement that I never expected to see in a pamphlet of this nature.

The author stated that if God is calling you to the priesthood or religious life, you will almost certainly have a desire for it. In other words, if the Lord wants you to become a priest, the first clue is that you'll *want to be a priest!* While it's possible that your other wants may cause you to ignore that desire, it should still be there initially, provided you've given it some thought and prayer.

You have no idea how relieved I was when I realized that I didn't have to become a priest! My lack of desire was an obvious sign. I had completely discounted it, but it really was the answer.

In an effort to please God, we sometimes overlook this important basic point. If you're called to be a nurse, you probably won't become nauseated at the thought of blood and germs. If you are trying to figure out if you should take a job as a roofer, a fear of heights should make you think twice. If you think you're called to be a special education teacher but lack patience and don't like being around children, please reconsider. As obvious as it sounds, this simple rule could spare you many sleepless nights!

Let's look at another situation in which I learned to use my head. I'm sure that many of you who are parents can relate to the situation.

When she was young, my daughter Mary would run very high fevers. On several occasions, her fever reached 105 degrees. I can assure you that the first time this happened, it didn't take Eileen and me very long to call the doctor. The doctor gave us some steps that would help to lower the fever. If these steps worked, we could avoid bringing Mary to the hospital emergency room and simply take her to the pediatrician's office the following day.

After dealing with Mary's fevers a few times, we knew what to do to get her temperature down. We could tell when to head for the emergency room and when we could wait until the following day to call the doctor. We would pray for our daughter to get better, but we also knew when it was time to take action. We used our God-given intelligence to deal with the problem.

RESPONSIBILITIES

I receive many e-mails from people asking me how to discover God's will for their lives. One of the most common questions is: "I feel that God is calling me to switch jobs. What should I do?"

Since this is a calling that I felt for many years, I know how frustrating the process can be. I recently discovered some e-mails that I sent when I was initially feeling the desire to work as a full-time Catholic evangelist. I was still working full-time in project management while running a part-time apostolate.

Here is an excerpt from one of those e-mails addressed to a popular Catholic evangelist. I sought advice for dealing with this crazy idea that had recently entered my mind:

> After reading your story, I felt I had to write and ask for your advice. I work in the financial world, but my joy is the evangelization and apologetics work that I do for Following the Truth. I know it's crazy, but I would really like to make Catholic evangelization my full-time job.
>
> I am fifty years old and have twelve-year-old twin girls and a wife. I can't simply quit my job, as I am the sole provider for my family. My question to you is this: Is it possible to earn a living by doing full-time ministry? Does one depend on donations? I just don't know how I could pay the bills without a "normal" job.
>
> Right now I am working full-time and doing my writing at night, but it gets very tiring sometimes! I keep hoping that someone will offer me a job as a Catholic writer, but I think I may be dreaming. Maybe I need to have someone tell me that I'm not being realistic, but I just can't get this desire out of my head. I'd appreciate any advice that you could send my way.

I'll keep your ministry in my prayers. Keep up the good work!

God bless,

Gary

This e-mail was composed three years before I became a full-time Catholic evangelist. It expresses some interesting ideas.

For one thing, notice that even though I believed God was calling me to work for him on a full-time basis, I was having a difficult time believing that he could provide for my family and me outside a "normal" (or conventional) job. In all honesty, it wasn't until several months into my new career that I truly started to believe that it was possible to earn a living in this manner (more on that later).

The main thing I want to point out about this e-mail, however, is my acceptance of the fact that I have to provide for the financial needs of my family. *I can't emphasize this enough!* If you feel that the Lord is calling you to change careers or leave your present job, but you have no way to pay your monthly bills, be careful. It's highly unlikely that the Lord will call you to do something that does not provide a way for you to meet your financial obligations. Jesus stated that "the laborer deserves his wages" (Luke 10:7), and St. Paul pointed out the need to "work in quietness" and earn a living (2 Thessalonians 3:12).

In the three years that I was trying to determine how I would pay the bills working as a full-time Catholic evangelist, I spoke with many individuals who had made the mistake, or knew people who had made the mistake, of leaving their jobs with the intention of doing God's will but had no way to support themselves financially. They cautioned me to avoid making this mistake. Although all things are possible with God and he does want us to trust him, he rarely asks us to do things that violate the principles of common sense.

Incidentally, the response I received to this e-mail—and it was sound advice—was to find some way to bring in income—either by donations, speaking, or writing books—before quitting my full-time job. It took a few years, but it was well worth the wait!

How about the "less important" decision of volunteering at church when you have family duties? While every case is different and requires some prayer and meditation, there is a basic rule that should guide us: Nothing is more important than our family responsibilities, not even volunteering at church or school. If our outside activities begin to adversely affect our family life, especially when we have young children, we should seriously consider cutting back so we can spend more time ministering to those God has entrusted to our care. Keep in mind the example of Jesus, who lived an uneventful life with Mary and Joseph when he was young.

Several years ago, I felt that the Lord might be calling me to become a permanent deacon. I discussed the matter with my pastor, who wisely encouraged me to wait until my children were older. As it turns out, I don't feel that the diaconate was ever God's plan for me but, rather, something that I wanted to do. That simple, commonsense piece of advice from my pastor proved to be worth its weight in gold.

What's Your Style?

It's also important that we identify our decision-making style. Some individuals are impulsive and frequently make decisions based on feelings. ("This just feels right, so I'm going to do it.") These people would definitely benefit from the "Does it make sense?" approach detailed in the previous paragraphs.

On the other hand, many people are extremely cautious when trying to reach a decision. They go through a great deal of analysis before acting. These people can take advantage of the technique as a first step in their process of making a decision.

We will have choices to make each day of our lives. Using our God-given intelligence can often help us to do the right thing without pursuing a long discernment process. Putting this into practice when I was in college would have spared me a great deal of agony, as I would have realized that someone who is not good with numbers should not be an accounting major! Fortunately, the Lord can bring good even out of the poor choices that we make.

Trying to determine what God wants us to do is a process that takes time. As you'll see in the rest of the book, however, it is a process that is quite doable if you're willing to put in some effort and follow some basic steps.

As Catholics, we believe that Jesus founded a Church to help us get to heaven. In the next chapter, we'll examine how the Church can help us to make decisions pleasing to the Lord.

KEY POINTS

1. We can often rule out potential choices simply because they don't make sense.
2. We have different responsibilities according to our state in life.
3. People make decisions in different ways. Some depend heavily on their feelings, and others rely more on logic and analysis.
4. Using our intelligence is only one part of making decisions in accordance with God's will, but it is an important step and shouldn't be ignored.
5. Although God wants us to make wise decisions, he can even bring good out of the bad choices that we make.

REFLECTION QUESTIONS

1. Do you generally give much thought to decision making, or do you tend to act impulsively?

2. Looking back over your life, have you ever made a decision that didn't make sense? Would you handle it differently today?

3. Do you feel God is calling you to make a major change in your life? How will it impact your family and current responsibilities?

4. Is there a difference between being cautious and not trusting in God's providence?

5. What is your initial reaction when faced with a big decision? Do you bring it to prayer?

Chapter Four

What Does Mother Church Say?

When making important decisions (those that affect our relationship with God), we can take comfort in a message that came directly from the lips of Jesus. Even though his words were spoken two thousand years ago, they are addressed to each one of us and reassure us of a very comforting fact:

> These things I have spoken to you, while I am still with you. But the Counselor, the Holy Spirit, whom the Father will send in my name, he will teach you all things, and bring to your remembrance all that I have said to you. (John 14:25–26)

Jesus knew that there would be times when we would feel alone. Those of us who are trying to seek his will are not exempt from this feeling. Fortunately for us, just because we may *feel* this way doesn't make it true. Feelings can be misleading. The fact of the matter is that Jesus *is* with us and will help us to make decisions that will please him.

One of the most basic (and underappreciated) ways that Jesus does this is through the teaching of his Church, which is guided by the Holy Spirit. According to the *Catechism of the Catholic Church*:

> So that she can fulfill her mission, the Holy Spirit "bestows upon [the Church] varied hierarchic and charismatic gifts, and in this way directs her." "Henceforward the Church, endowed with the gifts of her founder and faithfully observing

his precepts of charity, humility and self-denial, receives the mission of proclaiming and establishing among all peoples the Kingdom of Christ and of God, and she is on earth the seed and the beginning of that kingdom." (*CCC* 768, quoting *Lumen Gentium*, 4, 5)

Simply put, since the Holy Spirit, fulfilling Jesus's promise, guides the Church and protects her from teaching false doctrine, we can look to the Church for assistance when attempting to decide what God wants us to do. And not only can the Church provide assistance, but we can take her advice as coming directly from Jesus. We can have total confidence that we'll get sound advice.

I don't know about you, but that really puts my mind at ease. Even the advice of my good friends and confidants doesn't come with that kind of guarantee!

The Holy Spirit at Work

Let's examine the importance of the Holy Spirit's working through the Church. If we don't take some time to recognize just how logical this is, there's a chance that we could misinterpret Jesus's words about the Holy Spirit.

While there is no doubt that the Holy Spirit resides in each of us (that's a matter of Church teaching), he is active in the Church in a unique way. Through the Magisterium (or teaching office of the Church), the Holy Spirit assists us in following God's commandments. Although the idea of obeying the commands of the Lord sounds simple, many well-intentioned people go astray because they overlook the criticality of authoritative Church teaching.

Let's look at the question of birth control. Suppose I'm a good Christian man or woman who is sincerely trying to follow God's will, but I'm confused as to whether or not I should have another child. If money is tight and I already have several children, there's a good chance that I could arrive at the conclusion that having another child is not the right thing to do. I could sincerely believe that God is telling me that he doesn't want me to have another child and, further, that artificial contraception is the morally correct decision.

If we look at this decision in a vacuum, it can sound reasonable. After all, would it be fair to bring a new child into the world, given the fact that I can barely provide for my current family? On the other hand, another devout Christian could look at the same situation and decide that being open to another child is the correct thing. If we really trust God, we should believe that he will provide for our needs, correct?

Looking at these two choices, one could reasonably conclude that either is morally correct. Therein lies the danger of discounting the importance of Church teaching in the decision-making process. Jesus promised that the Holy Spirit will guide us into all the truth (see John 16:13). He does this through the teaching authority of the Catholic Church. When the Church speaks, it is Jesus himself who is speaking.

A Catholic who seeks to follow God's will can arrive at the right decision by looking at the Church's teaching. Even if one's intentions are noble, the practice of contraception is morally unacceptable (see *CCC* 2399). Therefore, it can safely be said that choosing that option would not be following God's will.

On the other hand, the Church does recognize the regulation of procreation as a responsibility for married couples. Further, the Church advises that Natural Family Planning is the proper means of carrying out this responsibility:

> Periodic continence, that is, the methods of birth regulation based on self-observation and the use of infertile periods, is

in conformity with the objective criteria of morality. These methods respect the bodies of the spouses, encourage tenderness between them, and favor the education of an authentic freedom. (*CCC* 2370; see *Humanae Vitae*, 16, 14)

How can we be so sure that this is God's will for married couples? Because Jesus speaks through his Church. He told his disciples, "Whatever you bind on earth shall be bound in heaven, and whatever you loose on earth shall be loosed in heaven" (Matthew 18:18). When faced with decisions on the hot-button issues of modern life—decisions involving the sanctity of life (abortion, euthanasia, in vitro fertilization), chastity (adultery, premarital sex, pornography, homosexuality), and truthfulness (lying, calumny, perjury), for example—the Church instructs us regarding which potential choices are moral. The *Catechism of the Catholic Church* is an excellent resource to consult when we are making moral decisions.

Several years ago, I was faced with a very difficult decision regarding my mother. After the death of my father, it was apparent that my mother was incapable of living by herself. She was beginning to forget things and would repeat herself constantly. A doctor confirmed that she was suffering from dementia, and he said that her forgetfulness was only going to get worse.

I tried to convince my mother that she should move to an assisted living facility, but Mom adamantly refused. Taking her for tours of various facilities and trying to put a positive spin on the move had no effect. My mother did not want to move.

I tried to pray and not worry. But one day, Mom asked a landscaper who came to her door looking for work to come in and fix her television set. Coupled with many other episodes, this lack of judgment moved me to take action. I decided that I would have to make up a story in order to get her to voluntarily leave the house.

On one hand, I felt that I was justified in lying. After all, I had to protect my mother from harm, and this seemed to be the only way. But the idea of lying didn't sit well with me. Even though it would be for her own good, I felt uncomfortable about lying to my mother.

I decided to consult the *Catechism*. Sure enough, the *Catechism* stated that "lying is to be condemned" (*CCC* 2485). Hoping there was an out for me because of my mother's condition, I contacted my pastor. When I explained the dilemma to him, he agreed with the Church's teaching and urged me to tell my mother the truth, albeit in a creative way. Although I didn't particularly *want* to hear this message, I *needed* to hear it.

Telling my mother the truth was indeed the best approach. Even though it made the process more difficult and drawn out, it was the correct thing to do, and the Lord allowed the situation to work out. And as usual, his timing was perfect. Shortly after arriving at the assisted living facility, my mother's mental condition worsened drastically. We are extremely fortunate that she is safe and well cared for to this day.

CONSCIENCE

What about the role of conscience in the decision-making process? Some will argue that conscience enables us to judge right from wrong, thereby making the teaching of the Church unnecessary. Often, Catholics will cite Church teaching on the conscience as the ultimate guide when making moral decisions.

While our conscience can be an effective tool in making the right choice, it is not infallible. Many individuals have followed their conscience and headed down a road that produced one evil act after another. Conscience does not replace the moral guidance of Church teaching.

What role, then, does our conscience play when we are trying to decide what God wants us to do?

> Moral conscience [see Romans 2:14–16], present at the heart of the person, enjoins him at the appropriate moment to do good and to avoid evil. It also judges particular choices, approving those that are good and denouncing those that are evil [Romans 1:32]. It bears witness to the authority of truth in reference to the supreme Good to which the human person is drawn, and it welcomes the commandments. When he listens to his conscience, the prudent man can hear God speaking. (*CCC* 1777)

At first glance, it can appear that conscience is all we need to make proper decisions. A statement from the *Catechism* might seem to strengthen that understanding: "A human being must always obey the certain judgment of his conscience. If he were deliberately to act against it, he would condemn himself" (*CCC* 1790).

When we look at the total picture, however, the true teaching emerges. While the Church is indeed asserting that we should obey the certain judgments of our conscience, the sentence that follows provides an important qualification: "Yet it can happen that moral conscience remains in ignorance and makes erroneous judgments about acts to be performed or already committed" (*CCC* 1790).

In spite of our good intentions, it is possible that our conscience can lead us to make wrong decisions. In other words, we can choose courses of action that do not please God. The Lord expects us to take the steps necessary to inform our conscience. How do we know this? Again, through the clear teaching of the Catholic Church:

This ignorance can often be imputed to personal responsibility. This is the case when a man "takes little trouble to find out what is true and good, or when conscience is by degrees almost blinded through the habit of committing sin." In such cases, the person is culpable for the evil he commits. (*CCC* 1791, quoting *Gaudium et Spes,* 16)

If we fail to inform our conscience, we will be held responsible on the day of our judgment. Simply saying, "I didn't know that contraception was a sin," might not be good enough.

How do we ensure that our conscience is informed? By turning to the teaching of the Church! Jesus told us that we express our love for him by keeping his commandments (see John 14:15). Why do many Catholics who claim to love Jesus ignore the teachings of his Church when making decisions? I can suggest a few reasons.

For one thing, many Catholics have a minimal knowledge of Church teaching. Despite twelve years of Catholic school, I was in that position for many years. I didn't know what the Church taught about many things, and I was too lazy to find out. Why? Primarily because it wasn't that important to me. While I'm not proud to admit that fact, it's a common way of thinking.

Another reason why "Jesus-loving Catholics" feel justified in ignoring the teachings of the Church is also rooted in a lack of understanding. Many Catholics do not see the association between Jesus and his Church. Instead of seeing a divine institution founded by Christ to help us get to heaven, they view the Church as a bureaucracy that is out of touch with reality. Viewing the Church in this way (or focusing on the public indiscretions of some of her leaders) usually leads to a cynical view of the Church that makes it easy to ignore her teachings.

JESUS AND HIS CHURCH

In order to obtain an accurate view of the relationship between Jesus and his Church, let's take a look at a famous encounter recorded in the pages of the Bible.

Two thousand years ago, Saul of Tarsus, better known by his Roman name of Paul, had an unforgettable meeting with Jesus on the road to Damascus (see Acts 9:1–19). As he fell to the ground, Saul heard a voice say, "Saul, Saul, why do you persecute me?" (Acts 9:4). When Saul inquired as to the identity of the speaker, he was told, "I am Jesus, whom you are persecuting" (Acts 9:5).

Saul thought that he was persecuting Christians (or the Church), but he was actually persecuting Jesus. Why? Because the Church is the Mystical Body of Christ. Paul went on to address this concept frequently in his letters, reminding us of how closely Jesus identifies with his Church:

> Now you are the body of Christ and individually members of it (1 Corinthians 12:27).

> [The Father] has made him the head over all things for the church, which is his body, the fullness of him who fills all in all (Ephesians 1:22–23).

> In [Christ] the whole fulness of deity dwells bodily, and you have come to fulness of life in him, who is the head of all rule and authority (Colossians 2:9–10).

Although the laity, clergy, and religious all make up the Church on earth, we have different roles. Beginning with the apostles (under the leadership of St. Peter), Jesus established a hierarchical Church structure with the power to speak authoritatively on matters of faith and morals. "God has appointed in the church first apostles, second prophets, third teachers, then workers of miracles, then healers, helpers, administrators, speakers in various kinds of tongues" (1 Corinthians 12:28). When the Church proclaims that contraception, in vitro fertilization, cohabitation, and drunkenness are sinful, it is truly Jesus who speaks.

Keeping that in mind can greatly simplify the process of making decisions according to God's will. Whenever we are trying to make a decision that pleases the Lord, any option that goes against Church teaching should immediately be discounted. *It is never God's will that we disobey the teachings of his Church.* If there was ever a rule that was written in stone, this is it!

KEY POINTS

1. When making decisions, we should always look to the teachings of the Church.
2. It is never God's will that we disobey the commands of his Church.
3. Although we should depend on our conscience to make moral decisions, our conscience can be faulty and cause us to choose an option that displeases God.
4. Our conscience should be formed in accordance with the teachings of the Church.
5. If we don't make reasonable efforts to inform our conscience, we are responsible for any resulting evils.

REFLECTION QUESTIONS

1. When making a decision, do you consider what the Church teaches?
2. If you encounter a difficult Church teaching, do you make an effort to understand it by doing more research?

3. Have you disagreed with a Church teaching in the past and changed your mind after studying the reasons behind it? Which teaching(s)?

4. What steps do you take to inform your conscience? Do you read the Catechism? Do you ever ask a priest for guidance?

5. If you disagree with a Church teaching, do you obey it anyway?

CHAPTER FIVE

Listen to Mother Mary

DO YOU EVER GET FRUSTRATED WHEN TRYING TO DETERMINE WHAT God wants you to do in a given situation? How about when trying to get his assurance that a future event will work out for the best? Over the course of my life, I have cried out several times, "Lord, just let me know what you want me to do already!"

Most of us feel uncomfortable when dealing with uncertainty and the unknown. That's one of the reasons why death can be such a frightening concept. We like guarantees and reassurances. When we invest our money, we generally prefer a guaranteed rate of return and protection against a major loss. When trying to follow God's will, sometimes the inability to see how it will turn out can cause us a great deal of anxiety.

Fortunately, there is someone who can help us with this situation. When it comes to surrendering to God's will without having all the answers, no one stands out the way our Blessed Mother does. By looking at Mary's life and asking for her assistance, we can learn to overcome many of the fears associated with following God's will, even when we can't see what the future will bring.

HOW CAN THIS BE?

We sometimes forget just how much uncertainty Mary had to endure. It's easy to overlook the fact that, although she was conceived without original sin and never committed a sin, she was every bit as human as we are. Even though she was handpicked by God to be the mother of the Messiah, she wasn't given all the answers up front. The Lord often spoke to her just as he speaks to us—in mystery.

Looking at her life as recorded in the Bible, however, reminds us of the many times she trusted God even when things didn't appear to make sense. Furthermore, her words and actions can provide us with valuable advice for seeking God's will when we're confused and unsure. If we follow her lead, we can learn to "walk by faith, not by sight" (2 Corinthians 5:7).

The first mention of Mary in the Bible tells of her famous encounter with the angel Gabriel. She was "greatly troubled" by his words "Hail, full of grace, the Lord is with you" (Luke 1:28–29). While you and I may struggle to find anything troubling in these words, Mary's humility caused her to be uncomfortable with the salutation. Interesting, isn't it?

Those who are humble can be uncomfortable receiving praise. Therefore, Mary's reaction is not at all surprising. What is surprising, however, is how she reacted to the angel's subsequent words. After being informed that she had found favor with God and would conceive and bear a son named Jesus, Mary was also told that her son would be the long-awaited Messiah (see Luke 1:30–33). She reacted not with disbelief or fear but by asking a simple question: "How can this be, since I have no husband?" (Luke 1:34).

Mary's question seems curious, to say the least. Mary was betrothed to Joseph. More than just an engagement, a betrothal was considered to be a legally binding marriage. The only difference was that the couple did not yet live together. Taking that into account, why would Mary be confused about the news that she was to bear a child? Isn't that what was expected of a young married woman?

Note that Mary didn't inquire about being the mother of the Savior, what we might consider the more difficult part of the message to understand. She was confused as to how she would be able to give birth. The only practical explanation of her confusion is that she had previously vowed to remain a virgin.

Giving no indication of any doubt on Mary's part, the angel proceeded to answer the question in an interesting manner:

> The Holy Spirit will come upon you,
> and the power of the Most High will overshadow you;
> therefore the child to be born will be called holy,
> the Son of God. (Luke 1:35)

While he certainly answered Mary's question, Gabriel gave no details as to what this would involve. There were no recommendations for explaining it to her family, no reassurances that the experience would be pleasant. And since Mary didn't ask about any of those things, Gabriel's lack of detail is completely understandable.

The one question that Mary asked tells us a great deal about her faith. The only piece of information she needed was how she could give birth and remain a virgin. Mary wanted to be sure that she was interpreting Gabriel's words correctly. She didn't doubt that God could take care of the details but wanted to know how to proceed.

When we attempt to determine what God wants us to do, asking questions is an important part of the process. However, not all questions are created equal. A few verses prior to Mary's encounter with Gabriel, Zechariah posed a similar question to the angel. After being told that his wife, Elizabeth, would bear a son, John the Baptist, the priest questioned the practicality of the news (see Luke 1:18). After all, both Zechariah and his wife were elderly, so the news didn't make sense.

Unlike Mary, who asked a question in order to better understand God's will, Zechariah asked a question of disbelief: "How shall I know this? For I am an old man, and my wife is advanced in years" (Luke 1:18). Even though he and his wife had prayed for a child (see Luke 1:13), he didn't believe that the Lord was granting the request.

The words of the angel confirm Zechariah's lack of faith: "You will be silent and unable to speak until the day that these things come to pass, because you did not believe my words, which will be fulfilled in their time" (Luke 1:20).

As we attempt to discover the Lord's will for us, it would be wise to imitate Mary and ask questions that help us to better follow his plan. Asking God how we can best serve him through unemployment, sickness, tragedy, and other periods of uncertainty is a great example of imitating Mary. We should feel comfortable asking for explanations when we are going through difficult periods in our lives.

It's important also that we be willing to accept an answer of "Trust me." Sometimes God's lack of a clear answer is a means for helping increase our faith in him.

Once Mary understood that her pregnancy would occur by the power of the Holy Spirit, she freely proclaimed her "yes" and had no further questions. How was she able to do that when a virgin birth is "impossible"? She believed the angel's words: "With God nothing will be impossible" (Luke 1:37). She was right.

Even though Mary was confused about Gabriel's message, it turned out that her discernment had been correct all along. The Lord *did* want her to remain a virgin, *and* he wanted her to have a child. Yet another reminder to trust the Lord at all times.

Looking for Jesus

Here is an often overlooked piece of advice: When trying to determine what God wants us to do, we should seek him out and remain

LISTEN TO MOTHER MARY

close to him. Makes perfect sense, doesn't it? If we are concerned about following the Lord's will, having a close relationship with him makes the process much simpler.

Unfortunately, we can get so wrapped up in the pros and cons of our potential choices that we forget to seek God's guidance as we make our decisions. Once again, the Blessed Mother comes to the rescue and gives us a plan to follow. In an event commonly referred to as the finding in the temple (see Luke 2:41–52), Mary teaches us a valuable lesson by her words and actions.

Every year, Mary and Joseph would make the trip to Jerusalem for the Feast of Passover. As documented in Scripture, one year proved to be quite memorable. When the feast was over, Mary and Joseph began the journey home, unintentionally leaving the twelve-year-old Jesus behind.

While this incident may make the couple seem irresponsible, there are some reasonable explanations for how this could have happened. During these pilgrimages, it was common for the men and the women to travel separately. Therefore, it's entirely possible that Mary thought Jesus was with her husband and Joseph thought he was with Mary. Another possibility is that the couple thought he was with family or friends. "Supposing him to be in the company they went a day's journey, and they sought him among their kinsfolk and acquaintances" (Luke 2:44).

Mary and Joseph discovered that Jesus was missing, so they returned to Jerusalem in search of him. When they discovered him in the temple, Mary asked Jesus: "Son, why have you treated us so? Behold, your father and I have been looking for you anxiously" (Luke 2:48).

Mary's words remind us of possibly the most important step we can take when trying to determine what the Lord wants us to do. Search for

· · · 45 · · ·

him! Instead of worrying that we'll make the wrong choice or taking matters completely into our own hands, we should seek the Lord and his wisdom. Furthermore, in Mary's own words, we shouldn't wait but should seek him *anxiously*!

After Jesus explained that he must be in his Father's house, St. Luke mentions that Mary and Joseph didn't understand their Son's words (see Luke 2:50). Even the mother and foster father of Jesus didn't have all the answers! Just like us, they sometimes found the Lord's message confusing. More importantly, however, Mary provides us with another important step in the process of seeking God's will. She "kept all these things in her heart" (Luke 2:51).

How do we respond when trying to make a difficult decision? Do we continuously bring it to prayer and seek to understand the Lord's will, or do we stop asking and try to handle the matter on our own? Prayerful contemplation was a frequent practice of the Blessed Mother (see Luke 1:29; 2:19). I can definitely attest to its effectiveness, and I strongly recommend it for anyone truly seeking God's will. Sometimes God's will is not immediately apparent. It can even appear that he has deserted us. During these times, perseverance is crucial.

During the almost three years that I was trying to determine if the Lord was calling me to work for him on a full-time basis, I had many ups and downs. I was miserable and overwhelmed in my job, which at this point had shifted from computer programming to project management. Yet, I didn't know how I could support my family without the income from that job. I knew I wanted to work as a full-time Catholic evangelist, but I wasn't sure if it was what God wanted me to do. As a result, I prayed—a lot!

One of my favorite lunchtime activities was to visit a local Cistercian monastery and converse with the Lord. As I walked around the calm and peaceful lake on the property, I spent many hours asking the Lord a simple question: "Why, Lord?" I couldn't figure out why the Lord would want me to continue working in a career that brought me a great deal of pain. Eventually, an answer came to me. While it's very likely that it wasn't the only reason, this potential reason brought me some comfort.

I realized that all of my earthly suffering would one day come to an end. It will certainly end when I die, but it may end much sooner. Taken by itself, that realization made me feel better.

Even more importantly, I was overcome with an urgent desire to offer up my suffering. While I should have thought of it sooner, I was probably too busy feeling sorry for myself to notice. I was wasting a golden opportunity to unite my suffering with the suffering of Christ, thereby sharing in his mission. What a tremendous privilege, and one that could vanish at any time.

Although nothing changed externally, *everything* changed for me! I had been asking the Lord several times a day for over a year why he was letting me go through this. Then he "suddenly" answered me.

Persistent and prayerful meditation is an incredibly effective tool for understanding God's will. Mary practiced it frequently, and I'm glad that I did too.

"Let It Be to Me"

In Mary's life, the pursuit of God's will sometimes required a decision and at other times required simple acceptance. While Mary certainly had to make a choice when visited by Gabriel and asked to become the mother of the Savior (let's not forget that she could have refused), other events in her life were simply matters of accepting God's will. Simeon's prophecy of the suffering she would endure (see Luke 2:35) comes to mind. Whether or not she was making an active decision, however,

Mary consistently demonstrated a willingness to submit to God's will. The fact that it often involved suffering did not deter Our Lady.

One of the greatest examples of this is her presence at the foot of the cross (see John 19:25). Her presence at Calvary is a powerful sign of her embrace of God's will. Mary carried her cross of emotional, mental, and spiritual pain, acquiescing to the Father's plan for the redemption of mankind.

Because of the fact that Mary never sinned and always followed God's will, we should seek to imitate her in our daily lives. Doing so will keep us on track and help us to determine what the Lord wants us to do. As important as her function as a role model is, however, Mary can be even more helpful as a friend and intercessor.

God chose Our Lady for a unique mission: to deliver the Savior to the world. She wants to bring you and Jesus closer together. Mary has a great desire to assist you in growing closer to her Son and to help you follow his will for your life.

As he was dying on the cross, Jesus gave us the gift of Mary as our spiritual mother (see John 19: 26–27). Please don't waste that tremendous gift. The Blessed Mother wants to help you understand and follow God's plan for your life. Ask her to help you.

Consider Mary's words at the wedding of Cana: "Do whatever he tells you" (John 2:5). Putting our mother's advice into practice has a twofold benefit. It will not only allow you to determine what God wants you to do in any given situation but will also get you to heaven!

Not a single word of Mary is recorded in the Bible after these words at Cana. Why? After giving us that advice, what else was there to say?

Mary always followed God's will and now resides in heaven. That should be our objective as well. Don't try to do it by yourself; it won't work. Instead, turn to your Blessed Mother and listen to her. She knows what she's talking about!

KEY POINTS

1. Although she was chosen to be the Mother of God, Mary was human and would sometimes be confused by the events in her life.

2. Mary's strong faith enabled her to trust God, even when it didn't make sense according to the world's standards.

3. Prayerfully meditating on the events in her life was a frequent practice of Our Lady.

4. More than just being an excellent spiritual role model, Mary also wants to pray for us and help us to grow closer to her Son.

5. Mary's last recorded words in the Bible, "Do whatever he tells you," remind us of the importance of always listening to Jesus.

REFLECTION QUESTIONS

1. Spend some time reflecting on the fact that Mary was human and didn't have all the answers. Does it bring you comfort to know that she had to discern God's will in the same way that we do?

2. Put yourself in Mary's place when Gabriel announced that she had been chosen to become the mother of the Savior. How would you feel?

3. What questions would you have asked the angel in the above situation? Would you ask for any promises or guarantees?

4. When facing a difficult decision or enduring an unpleasant situation, do you bring it to prayer? Do you ask the Lord for enlightenment?

5. Have you accepted Jesus's gift of Mary as your spiritual mother?

Chapter Six

Listening for the Still, Small Voice

O that today you would hearken to his voice!

—Psalm 95:7

LET'S FACE IT: WE LIVE IN A VERY NOISY WORLD. RADIO, TELEVISION, and the Internet provide an endless stream of noise; MP3 players, cell phones, and other portable devices can take it to the next level. We can literally listen to something wherever we go, and many of us take advantage of this technical phenomenon.

Need proof? Take note of the people you see walking or jogging. How often do you see someone without earphones?

We have become so accustomed to noise that we can feel bored or lonely when we're not listening to something. The noise becomes a source of comfort.

In my younger days, I used to fall asleep listening to talk radio. I liked the sound of people talking, and I couldn't go to sleep without it. Interestingly, the noise was more important than the subject matter. When things were too quiet, I felt alone, and my mind would begin to race. Noise was my companion.

Don't get me wrong. Audio and visual media can be very useful; they shouldn't be dismissed entirely. My major conversion was helped greatly by Catholic radio and television. Now I spend a great deal of time speaking about Jesus on various media outlets, which are tremendous evangelization tools. I'll take it a step further and say that it's entirely possible for the Lord to speak through the media.

The fact remains, however, that there are many voices in the world that compete with God's voice. If we are serious about doing his will, we must come up with a way to distinguish the Lord's voice from all of the competing voices. After all, how can we obey him if we're unable to hear him?

Are you able to recognize God's voice when he speaks to you? While at first it may seem overwhelming, rest assured that it is possible. Jesus confirms this: "My sheep hear my voice, and I know them, and they follow me" (John 10:27).

The Shepherd's Voice

While Jesus's words provide assurance that we *can* hear his voice, how can we be sure that we're hearing him and not someone else? After all, making a mistake and following the wrong voice could have serious consequences. "Beware of false prophets," Jesus warned, "who come to you in sheep's clothing but inwardly are ravenous wolves" (Matthew 7:15).

The most effective way to recognize the voice of Jesus is by getting to know him personally. Indeed, knowing Jesus is essential if we want to follow him and get to heaven. It really is *that* important!

In a sense, a personal relationship with Jesus is similar to any other relationship. My wife and I have been married for twenty years, and she knows me very well. As a result, she generally has a good idea of how I will react in a given situation. There have been times when she has told me that she could hear what I would say even though I wasn't there. Conversely, I can sometimes hear Eileen speak to me even when she is not physically present.

One situation that comes to mind is mowing the grass. I like to push myself in order to get finished, so I generally don't like to take breaks and drink water, even if it's very warm outside. Because she loves me and cares about my well-being, Eileen will remind me to stop and get something to drink. It's gotten to the point where I can almost hear her reminders while I'm mowing. And as a result, I take periodic breaks from my work even when she's not around.

Because Eileen and I have a close relationship, I am also very aware of what she would *not* say. She would never recommend doing something unethical, for example. No risk of entertaining thoughts about cheating on our income taxes with her voice in my brain!

In the same way, a close personal relationship with Jesus will enable us to know what he would say and what he would not say. I can assure you with absolute certainty that Jesus will never tell you that it's acceptable to hate your enemies or to entertain impure thoughts. If you feel that he is telling you to do something immoral, there's no need to discern further. You are *not* hearing the voice of Jesus!

For many years, I thought I was a good Catholic (mainly because I went to Mass each week), but I justified many sinful actions by using the weak arguments that "God gave me these desires," "It's no big deal," or "Everyone does it." It's amazing how many sins I could excuse with these lines of reasoning. As my relationship with the Lord grew, however, I realized just how wrong I was. The better we get to know Jesus, the more we will understand how he wants us to behave.

Besides the black and white cases of choosing between good and evil, there are other situations in which God might want to direct us. How about trying to choose between two potential job offers or deciding on which house to purchase? Just because none of the options are evil doesn't mean that Jesus doesn't have a preference for which option you choose. Unless the decision is a minor one, it's quite possible that he does care. While we may not know with absolute certainty (more on that in the next chapter), we can be reasonably sure what he wants us to do by listening to his voice.

Open My Ears, Lord

If it were up to me, I would ask the Lord to speak to me in a loud, clear, booming voice. In that way, I could be absolutely sure that he is speaking and know exactly what he wants me to do. Somehow, I suspect that many of you feel the same way. If we turn to the Bible, we'll see that we're not alone in thinking that way. The prophet Elijah sought the Lord in the great wind, an earthquake, and a fire but ultimately encountered him in a "still small voice" (see 1 Kings 19:9–13).

Looking at it from a purely human perspective, the Lord *should* speak to us in a loud and clear voice. It would save time and leave little room for misinterpretation. But if we look at it from God's perspective, we can see the benefits of his speaking in a more mysterious way.

For one thing, the time we spend seeking to hear and understand the voice of the Lord is time spent in his presence. This time permits us to get to know him better. Human nature being what it is, if we got our answer quickly and directly, there's a very good chance that we wouldn't feel the need to continually converse with the Lord. This could result in our spending less time with him, which would prove detrimental to our relationship.

Seeking God in mystery also teaches us patience. It helps us understand that he is the Creator and we are the creatures. Rather than complain about God's method of communication, we would be wise to accept the fact that he gets to choose the best technique. Our job is to listen carefully to what he has to say!

So how does God speak to us? We've already covered some basic ways—our intellect and his Church. Sometimes he will use audible words, most often coming from other people. Other times he will put thoughts in our minds, feelings in our hearts, or visual images in our dreams. Some of his methods can be unconventional and easily over-looked. The Lord of the universe wants to speak to us and has many means at his disposal.

NATURE

Nature provides a powerful channel of divine communication. Unfortunately, we often fail to hear God speaking to us in this manner because we're used to verbal communication. Bible passages and homilies may be confusing at times, but we generally recognize that the Lord can speak to us through them because these methods use a traditional means of communication—words. The nonverbal communication of nature can be a bit more challenging. Although it may require some work on our part, we can often hear the Lord's voice clearly speaking through nature.

When we were first married, Eileen and I struggled with infertility. Although we wanted to have a large family, it was not happening. While we would never pursue any methods that went against Church teaching, we did meet with a doctor who specialized in infertility.

Initially, we were nervous. We feared that we would only be offered methods that we'd have to decline, such as in vitro fertilization. Much to our surprise, however, the doctor completely understood our religious beliefs. He recommended a simple test that would check for abnormalities in Eileen's uterus and fallopian tubes. He also informed us that sometimes the test could itself clear out debris in the tubes and make pregnancy possible. We left the doctor's office feeling very hopeful.

On the way home, Eileen called attention to something that confirmed our hopefulness. There was a beautiful rainbow in the sky. I immediately remembered that "with God nothing will be impossible" (Luke 1:37). While we didn't know for sure if we would be able to have children, we clearly heard God reminding us that it was possible. The Lord used that rainbow to convey a powerful message.

As someone with a tendency to be anxious, I have always sought out Bible verses that would remind me of the uselessness of worry. One of my favorites comes from Jesus's Sermon on the Mount: "Look at the birds of the air: they neither sow nor reap nor gather into barns, and yet your heavenly Father feeds them. Are you not of more value than they?" (Matthew 6:26).

This is the perfect message for those of us who sometimes lose sight of the Lord's providence. If God provides for the birds, why wouldn't he provide for us as well? While it's an obvious message, it's one that we can easily forget when we're faced with the problems of daily life. Every time I hear the birds chirp (and I'm hearing them as I write this), Jesus speaks these words to me, reminding me of his providential care.

Psalm 19 reminds us of how the Lord clearly speaks through creation.

> The heavens are telling the glory of God;
>> and the firmament proclaims his handiwork.
> Day to day pours forth speech,
>> and night to night declares knowledge.
> There is no speech, nor are there words;
>> their voice is not heard;
> yet their voice goes out through all the earth,
>> and their words to the end of the world. (Psalm 19:1–4)

PRAYER

I have to be honest and tell you that I've always struggled with the idea of God speaking to me in prayer. It wasn't until a few years ago that I started to understand why it was so difficult for me. As can be expected, the problem was on my end and not on the Lord's.

One of the biggest obstacles that I face when I pray is my tendency to do all the talking. As a result, I don't give the Lord a chance to speak. If I never stop talking, it's not easy for me to hear what God is saying. Makes sense, doesn't it?

Although it's not easy and requires some behavior modification on our part, we need to incorporate some silence into our prayer lives. When we do, we will hear God speak. While he may not necessarily speak in an audible manner, he most definitely will speak!

As discussed throughout this chapter, the Lord often speaks without using words. While it is possible that we can literally hear his voice, most of us don't. Instead, we'll get a thought or experience a feeling. This silent message will offer encouragement or make us feel that we should do something. Although it may be initially uncomfortable to listen to the Lord speaking in silence, it gradually gets easier.

There are times when the Lord's message is simply a feeling of peace. This is a very appropriate message for him to deliver. Remember, his first words to the apostles after he rose from the dead were "Peace be with you" (John 20:19).

Now, the obvious question that needs to be addressed is: "How do I know if it's the Lord speaking? What if it's just my thoughts?"

Throughout this book, I've emphasized that knowing Jesus personally is critical when trying to determine if it's his voice that you hear. As you grow closer to him, you will more clearly recognize his voice—even when he speaks in silence!

Obviously, a thought that you should commit a crime or disobey a teaching of the Church couldn't possibly come from Jesus, even if it occurs during prayer. On the other hand, I wouldn't spend an excessive amount of time trying to determine whether the "I love you" message really came from Jesus or from your own mind. In either case, it's a message that Jesus wants you to know and believe.

THE BIBLE

I always enjoy opening my talks with some good news: God is going to speak to you today! Although the initial reaction is generally one of disbelief, people begin to smile and nod their heads when they realize that I'm about to read from the pages of the Bible. Anyone who states that "God never speaks to me" (and that has probably been each of us at one time or another) should remember what the Church teaches about the Bible: "[I]n the sacred books, the Father who is in heaven meets his children with great love and speaks with them."[2]

If you want to let God speak to you and be certain that it is he who is speaking, the most effective thing to do is open up the Bible. Whether you're reading from the Old or New Testament doesn't matter. *Every time we read the Bible, God speaks directly to us.*

Is it possible that we could misinterpret what God is saying in the Bible? Absolutely! That's why it's important to familiarize ourselves with Church teaching (remember what you read in chapter 4) and not attempt to read the Bible in a vacuum.

PEOPLE

Few of you will be surprised to learn that God often speaks to us through other people. What may surprise you, or at least make you pause to think, is that he often uses unlikely individuals to deliver his message. While someone who is close to the Lord is probably more inclined to deliver his message accurately, God can use anyone as an instrument.

When I was trying to determine whether I should work full-time for the Lord, I spoke and corresponded with many individuals. I asked some people for advice (see my e-mail excerpt in chapter 3) and asked others for prayers. Some of the responses that I received were very surprising.

After asking someone involved in Catholic media to pray for me and expressing the feeling that I felt called to work for the Lord on a full-time basis, I was told, "Be thankful that you have a job." Another person in Catholic radio informed me that it probably wasn't God's will for me if I had to work too hard at making it happen. On the other hand, I received several encouraging messages from other individuals, assuring me of their prayers and expressing their opinion that I was being called to full-time ministry.

Since I was getting conflicting messages, how could I determine which, if any, of these opinions came from the Lord? Ultimately, I discovered that not all messengers are created equal. Some people were generally negative and cynical, while others were positive and hopeful. As an initial rule of thumb, though not as the sole means of discernment, I gave more credibility to the generally optimistic individuals. And when some of those folks told me that I should probably give it some more time, I took their advice very seriously.

While hearing the Lord is not an exact science, I recommend that you remain open to the possibility of God speaking to you through others. Let their advice factor into the decision-making process.

CIRCUMSTANCES

Sometimes the Lord speaks to us through the ordinary circumstances that occur in our daily lives. God often communicates through painful events, such as job loss, illness, and death. We can also hear his voice in pleasant occurrences, such as promotions, miraculous healings, and unexpected good news.

I still remember when I first met my wife. I was single and in my thirties, and she was the girl of my dreams. The only problem was that she was engaged to be married to someone else! I was extremely frustrated that the Lord would allow me to meet the perfect woman who happened to be completely unavailable.

Eileen and I were both involved in various Church activities, and we got to know each other very well. Even though it wasn't easy, I accepted the fact that our relationship would never progress beyond a certain level. One day, however, Eileen revealed some shocking news to me. There were some major problems with her relationship, and she was preparing to break off the engagement!

I was completely blown away and didn't know what to say or do. (Eileen, by the way, had no idea about my interest in her.) One thing led to another, and one year later, Eileen and I were married. This series of events left us with no doubt that the Lord wanted us to be together.

On January 6, 2012, I was laid off from my full-time job as a project manager. It was the first time in my thirty-year career that I had experienced a job layoff. The fact that my wife and I had been praying about the possibility of working for the Lord on a full-time basis didn't take away the sting.

Initially, I experienced the emotions of fear and rejection, but I was soon filled with peace. I clearly heard the Lord speak to me in this event. And as I look back, I realize it was one of the greatest days of my life, as it launched my career as a full-time Catholic author and evangelist.

God speaks to us in many ways, some conventional and some unconventional. If we are truly seeking his will for our lives, it behooves us to make the effort to hear his voice. While it may require turning off the noise that surrounds us, the reward will be great. We will be able to know his will and experience his peace.

Key Points:

1. God often speaks to us without using words.

2. The Lord's voice can be heard in nature, prayer, the Bible, other people, and circumstances.

3. Having a close personal relationship with Jesus is the best way to recognize his voice.

4. If we expect to hear God's voice, we must spend some time in silence.

5. The Lord speaks to us every time we read the Bible.

Reflection Questions:

1. Do you make an effort to converse with the Lord every day? Do you give him a chance to speak?

2. In what way (nature, prayer, Bible, people, circumstances) does God speak to you most often? In what way does he rarely speak to you?

3. Are you able to recognize the Lord's voice when he speaks? How can you be sure that it's really he who is speaking?

4. Would you say that you know Jesus well? Are you closer to him than you were last year?

5. Do you take time for silent prayer each day?

Chapter Seven

Direction and Discernment

Let's suppose that you have a major decision to make. Whether you're contemplating a job offer, a move to a new city, marriage, religious life, what college to attend, or any life-changing action, you shouldn't choose hastily. Furthermore, if you're trying to follow God's will, you should ask him what he wants you to do.

Perhaps you've applied all of the principles we've discussed so far, but you are still unsure which option best pleases the Lord. You've used your intellect, followed the Church's teachings, asked Mary for help, and listened for God's quiet voice, but some questions remain:

Is God really speaking to me?

How can I be sure?

What is he saying?

In chapter three of this book, we discussed the importance of using our intellect in following the Lord's will. As helpful and important as this is, however, it can also get in the way if we rely on it excessively. To put it bluntly, we can become too smart for our own good. It is entirely possible that God is asking us to do something we dismiss as impossible. That was exactly how I responded to the feeling that I was being called to full-time Catholic evangelism.

While God wants us to use common sense, he also wants us to walk by faith. Learning where to draw the line between using our intelligence and walking by faith can be confusing.

Another obstacle to discovering God's will is our own will. We sometimes hear the Lord asking us to do something but ignore the idea because it involves leaving our comfort zone. Due to our fallen human nature, we are all affected by some degree of inordinate self-love. Simply put, we have a tendency to prefer our own will over God's will.

So, what can we do? Fortunately, there are some steps we can follow that will greatly improve our ability to hear the Lord's voice and understand his message.

ADVICE FROM ST. IGNATIUS OF LOYOLA

Anyone who is facing a major decision should become acquainted with *The Spiritual Exercises of St. Ignatius of Loyola*. While the book can be intimidating and is primarily written for retreat leaders, it provides many helpful guidelines and recommendations to facilitate the discernment of God's will.[3] We'll take a closer, simplified look at St. Ignatius's rules for discernment later in this chapter, but here are some of his general concepts.

Ignatius states that, first of all, we need to know God in order to make decisions in accordance with the Lord's will.[4] As a result, many of the exercises consist of reading and reflecting on the life of Christ as recorded in the Gospels. As we've already discussed, getting to know Jesus is essential if we want to make decisions that will please him. The first step in getting to know him is learning the facts about his life— what he did and what he said. The Gospels provide an excellent means of acquiring that knowledge.

Ignatius also emphasizes the need to have a disposition to do God's will above all else.[5] While that sounds obvious, it's a principle that we violate frequently. We seek to follow God's will but give up when it becomes uncomfortable or conflicts with our own desires. I may have a desire to serve the Lord by being kind to others, but that desire may fade when people begin to annoy me.

How can we cultivate a desire to please God above all else? The answer is so simple that it can easily be overlooked: Get to know him better, and ask him for help! While it's just about impossible to change on our own, all things are possible with God. Praying for a decrease in self-love and an increase in the desire to follow his will can be very effective.

While we're on the subject of asking for help, let's discuss another important principle. St. Ignatius designed the Spiritual Exercises to be presented by a retreat leader. We shouldn't try to figure out God's will without seeking help from others. No matter how careful we are, we can fail to hear God's voice. Furthermore, we can misinterpret his message or respond to it in an incorrect manner. One of the best ways to ensure that we don't fall into these traps is to consult with another person.

SPIRITUAL DIRECTION

One of my favorite Bible stories involves Samuel and Eli (see 1 Samuel 3:1–18). It illustrates the importance of consulting with others when trying to hear and respond to the Lord's voice.

Samuel was a young boy who was assisting an elderly priest named Eli. One night while they were both lying down, Samuel heard a voice calling him. Thinking it was Eli's voice, the boy ran to the priest and replied, "Here I am!" Eli denied that he was calling Samuel and sent him away. Again the boy heard his name called and presented himself to Eli. He was once again told, "I did not call you," and instructed to lie down.

When called a third time, Samuel responded in the same way. Finally, Eli realized that it could be the Lord who was calling the boy, and he gave Samuel instructions for responding if he was called again. Samuel was to reply, "Speak, Lord, for your servant hears." When the

Lord called once again, the future prophet responded and was given an important mission.

By himself, Samuel didn't know how to recognize or respond to the Lord's voice. With the help of the more experienced Eli, however, the boy was able to hear and follow God's instructions.

While God can certainly speak through anyone, his message is more accurately delivered by those who know him well. When choosing a person to confirm something the Lord is telling you, a holy priest would be a better choice than an atheist. Why? Because he's closer to the Lord and is more familiar with his ways.

A spiritual director is someone who can assist you in seeking God's will. It can be a priest, deacon, religious sister, or lay person. One of the main benefits of spiritual direction is that it helps to neutralize the subjectivity that often creeps into the decision-making process.

My spiritual director was invaluable when I was attempting to decide whether the Lord was calling me to work for him full-time. When I began to read too much into events or let my mind run away, my spiritual director would help to reel me in and get me back on track.

While spiritual direction is not mandatory for those trying to follow God's will, it can be extremely helpful. If you don't have a spiritual director and would like one, I recommend that you ask the Lord to send one to you. It would also be a good idea to check with your local diocese, where you might find a list of qualified spiritual directors.

For more information about the process and benefits of spiritual direction, I highly recommend Dan Burke's book *Navigating the Interior Life*. In addition to explaining the concept of spiritual direction, this book will help you determine whether you need spiritual direction, help you find a spiritual director, and offer suggestions for what to do if you can't find a qualified one.

Steps to Heaven

As promised, let's now explore the step-by-step approach to decision making designed by St. Ignatius of Loyola. This method assumes that you have several options before you, none of which are evil, and that you are attempting to choose the one that will please God the most. Since it includes steps that take time, it is not recommended for decisions that have to be made quickly. (We'll discuss guidelines for making quick decisions in chapter 13.)

I also have to caution you that this is a greatly simplified version of the method taught by Ignatius in his Spiritual Exercises. If you are trying to make a major decision, you may wish to attend an Ignatian retreat. The length of such retreats can range from a weekend all the way up to thirty days. A retreat consists of a series of preparatory exercises preceding the decision-making steps. The steps we are about to cover, however, may provide all that you need to make a decision that conforms to God's will.

I found this method extremely helpful in making my decision to work for the Lord. After my job layoff in 2012, I spent several months trying to decide what I should do. Thanks to these steps, my decision became crystal clear. I'm thankful that St. Ignatius developed this method.

Before beginning the process, you should commit yourself to three things:[6]

1. You must be willing to choose the option that God wants, even if it's not what you want.
2. You must desire above all to please God, and your choice should reflect that desire.
3. You must immediately rule out any options that are immoral or go against Church teachings.

Now let's look at the three modes of discernment developed by St. Ignatius of Loyola.[7] They are designed to be used in order. If the first mode doesn't provide clear direction, then move on to the second. Only if that doesn't work, should you utilize the third mode.

Incidentally, there are two different methods for the third mode of discernment. The second way should only be used if the first doesn't provide clarity.

First Mode (No Doubt)
You positively know that one of the options is God's will and have no doubts at all.

This mode is hard to explain, but generally you will understand it when it happens. It occurs when you feel completely drawn to an option, and you simply *know* that it's God's will. If the Lord speaks to you in this way, it happens quickly, and there is no need to dwell on it. St. Ignatius likens this mode to the responses of St. Matthew and St. Paul when first called by Jesus. They experienced no doubt and followed the Lord without hesitation (see Matthew 9:9; Acts 9:1–19).

Second Mode (Heart's Desire)
St. Ignatius recommends that we dwell on the second mode if we don't receive clarity beyond doubt in the first mode. Slightly more complex, this mode of discernment involves consolations (spiritual joy, love, hope in things above, strong desire to pray) and desolations (sadness, lack of love, spiritual dryness, difficulty in prayer). Consolations and desolations are normal parts of the spiritual life and can be very useful in discerning God's will.

In another work, Ignatius recommends that a person attentively observe "when he finds himself in consolation, to which part [option] God moves him, and likewise when he finds himself in desolation."[8] For example, if you are trying to decide between keeping your current job and accepting a new offer, determine which job attracts you during periods of consolation and which attracts you during periods of desolation. If you repeatedly feel called to keep your current job during periods of consolation, there's a good chance that this is what God wants you to do. Additionally, during periods of desolation, you should expect to feel a call to the opposite choice.

The key is to be patient. This mode of discernment could take months or even years. Look for a recurring pattern.

Third Mode (Pros and Cons)

If the first two methods don't reveal God's will, it's time to move on to the third mode of discernment. St. Ignatius recommends that this mode be used during periods of tranquility, when the soul is at peace and free from passions that might influence a decision.

This method involves making a list of the pros and cons of each option. These pros and cons should be spiritually based, not based on personal preferences such as financial considerations or level of comfort. Once you create this list, there are two ways to arrive at a decision.

First Way of the Third Mode

1. Place before yourself the various options.
2. Putting aside your own personal desires, express your willingness to choose the option that will bring greater glory to God.
3. Ask the Lord to move you toward the option that will bring him greater glory.
4. Consider the spiritual pros and cons of each option.
5. After carefully pondering the spiritual advantages and disadvantages of each option, make a decision about which one will give greater glory to God.
6. Turn to the Lord in prayer and offer your choice to him, asking him to confirm it by granting you peace.

As a reminder, the second way of the third mode should only be used if sufficient clarity isn't provided by the first way.

Second Way of the Third Mode

1. You must desire to make your choice solely out of love for God.
2. How would you advise a person you've never met if he or she were faced with the same choice? Choose that option.
3. Picture yourself at the moment of your death. Which option would you be more inclined to choose? Choose that option.
4. Imagine you are standing in the presence of the Lord on the day of your judgment. Which option do you wish you had chosen? Choose that option.
5. Make your choice and present it to the Lord.
6. Ask the Lord to confirm your choice by granting you his peace.

The above methods are designed to help us remember that we are created to know, love, and serve God. St. Ignatius's first principle and foundation states: "Man is created to praise, reverence, and serve God our Lord, and by this means to save his soul."[9] By always making decisions with that principle in mind, we will not only please God but greatly increase our chances for getting to heaven.

Too often we become overly attached to created things. We become obsessed with people, possessions, and comfort and ignore the fact that God should come first in our lives. Properly using the above methods when making major decisions will greatly assist you in overcoming that tendency to self-love and allow you to focus on loving God before all else.

Please remember that discernment can be a complicated process and can take a long time. If you are patient, these methods will guide you to the options that please God the most. If you get frustrated, remember the pleasant byproduct that a lengthy discernment process can produce: a deeper relationship with the Lord. Time spent with the Lord is never wasted. The more we pray and encounter him, the better we will get to know him. That is always a good thing.

Key Points

1. When making decisions, love of God should be our primary goal.
2. We often become overly attached to people and possessions, which can cause us to ignore the Lord.
3. Reading and meditating on the Gospels is an excellent method for coming closer to Christ.
4. When facing a major decision, determining God's will can take months or even years.
5. Sometimes God's will involves doing things that we would rather avoid.

Reflection Questions

1. What is your basis for making decisions—to please God or to avoid discomfort?
2. Think of the most important things in your life. Do any of them get in the way of your relationship with the Lord?
3. Did you ever experience a deep sense of peace after making a decision? How about a lack of peace?
4. When making a big decision, do you ask friends for advice? If you receive conflicting opinions, how do you decide to whom you should listen?
5. How do you react when God doesn't answer quickly? Do you continue to pray? Do you become annoyed or stop praying? Do you trust that God's timing is perfect?

Chapter Eight

Take Your Time

I HAVE TO ADMIT THAT I'M AN IMPATIENT PERSON. ONCE I MAKE UP my mind that I want something, I don't like to wait. "Lord, give me patience—and I want it *now*."

When I started taking guitar lessons at the age of ten, I quickly grew bored with music theory and other basic knowledge. I wanted to play popular songs, and I wanted to be in a band. So I started learning how to play songs by ear, skipping the "boring" fundamentals. This caused me a great deal of difficulty several years later, when I was playing in a wedding band and struggling to read sheet music.

Another example of my impatience occurred during my college years. Frustrated with being too thin, I began lifting weights in the hope of becoming muscular. As the weeks passed and I couldn't see substantial results, I lost interest and eventually stopped exercising. Once again, my impatience proved to be my undoing. If I had persevered, keeping my eye on the prize, I would have probably been successful.

Unfortunately, many of us approach discerning God's will with the same lack of patience. Not only can that cause us a great deal of frustration and anxiety, but it can also have major repercussions in our lives. The Lord often takes his time in making his will known. A friend of mine once commented that it's a good thing that God doesn't drive an ambulance or a fire truck. Like it or not, the Lord has his own schedule, and sometimes we just have to wait for him.

PATIENT PEOPLE

Learning to be patient is something we must do if we want to hear God's voice and do his will. The Bible gives an example of how patience can definitely pay off:

> A woman who had had a flow of blood for twelve years and had spent all her living upon physicians and could not be healed by any one, came up behind him, and touched the fringe of his garment; and immediately her flow of blood ceased. (Luke 8:43–44)

Can you imagine spending twelve years and all of your money seeking a cure for a physical ailment? Most of us would have given up and considered the situation hopeless. The woman in this story did not do that, however. She approached Jesus in the hope of being cured. What would have happened if she had given up after one, two, or eleven years? While I can't say for sure, there's a very good chance that the cure would not have taken place.

This woman didn't give up. She believed that a cure was possible, and she continued to pursue it. She made the most of her encounter with the Lord, and her patience and persistence were rewarded as Jesus granted her unspoken request.

For thousands of years, the Israelites awaited the coming of the Messiah. Generation after generation of individuals passed on without seeing the arrival of the Savior. What took so long? Wasn't there a desperate need for him to arrive?

In his infinite wisdom, God had other plans: "When the time had fully come, God sent forth his Son, born of woman, born under the law, to redeem those who were under the law, so that we might receive adoption as sons" (Galatians 4:4–5).

St. Peter states that "with the Lord one day is as a thousand years, and a thousand years as one day" (2 Peter 3:8), and most of us will agree! It's not easy waiting on the Lord, especially when we need an answer in a hurry. Sometimes our pride lets us forget that we don't always know what's best for us. We may think we know what we need and when we need it, but we could be wrong. God is never wrong; he always knows what's best for us.

Let's face it, there will be situations in our lives and the lives of others that just don't make sense. God's ways are often unconventional, a fact that he made clear to the prophet Isaiah:

> For my thoughts are not your thoughts,
>> neither are your ways my ways, says the LORD.
> For as the heavens are higher than the earth,
>> so are my ways higher than your ways
>> and my thoughts than your thoughts. (Isaiah 55:8–9)

While none of us would claim to be smarter than God, our actions often send a different message. We complain when things don't go our way or when the Lord doesn't answer our prayers quickly enough. We know in our brains that the Lord knows what he's doing, but really trusting him in our day-to-day situations is challenging.

Jesus tells us that we need to become like children in order to get to heaven (see Matthew 18:3), which means that we need to trust that our heavenly Father knows what he's doing. I've always found Psalm 131 to be effective in reminding me that some things are just beyond my understanding. It's a good one to highlight in your Bible.

> O LORD, my heart is not lifted up,
>> my eyes are not raised too high;

I do not occupy myself with things
    too great and too marvelous for me.
But I have calmed and quieted my soul,
    like a child quieted at its mother's breast;
    like a child that is quieted is my soul.
O Israel, hope in the LORD
    from this time and for evermore. (Psalm 131)

CONFESSIONS OF A DEACON WANNA-BE

As I mentioned earlier, after having a major conversion in 2004, I started to take my Catholic faith very seriously. Reading, praying, listening to Catholic radio, and attending Mass became my daily routine. As I grew closer to the Lord, I wanted to serve him and share the Good News with others.

At the time, I thought the best way to do this was to become a permanent deacon. It was my belief that in order to become "really holy" I needed some sort of official title. Even though I didn't know what deacons did during the week, I saw them on Sunday, and they looked like holy men of God. Since holiness was my goal, the diaconate seemed like a good fit for me. I discussed the matter with my wife, and she agreed that it would be a good idea.

One day, as I was taking a walk and praying the rosary, I decided to call my pastor and inform him of my desire. My mind raced as I pictured his joyful reaction to my proclamation. I was nervous about making the call, but I felt it was the right thing to do.

Once I reminded Father of who I was (he only knew me from seeing my family and me on Sundays), I gave him the good news. He proceeded to tell me about the formation process. I was stunned. Not only would I have to attend class two times a week for four years, but my wife was also expected to participate. This would definitely pose a problem. Our daughters were only seven years old at the time, and Eileen and I both had many responsibilities at home.

Father was very understanding. He suggested that it might be better to wait until the girls were a bit older. I was crushed! I wanted to serve the Lord as a deacon, and I wanted to get started right away.

For the next several years, I anxiously looked forward to the day when my girls would be older and I could pursue my dream of becoming a permanent deacon. I have to confess that I spent a few back-to-school nights lamenting the fact that my children were still young. I found myself counting the years I'd have to wait before Eileen and I could attend the formation classes. Every time I saw one of the permanent deacons at church, I'd be envious. And I'm not proud to admit that I looked at other men who were active in the parish and hoped that they didn't beat me to it and take one of the open deacon slots.

While I may have started out with good intentions, my pursuit of the permanent diaconate became more about me and less about God. The desire to serve the Lord in this way turned into a quest for personal satisfaction. I was so busy looking to the future that I ignored the present. Somehow, I missed the point that the Lord had blessed me with a wonderful wife and children and that taking care of them was my primary vocation.

Fortunately, I realized that what I was doing was wrong. As a result, I embraced my role as a father and husband and learned to focus on the present moment. I also became involved in parish ministries that didn't adversely affect my family life. Along with this change came a sense of peace.

Looking back, I realize that I had a poor understanding of the role of the clergy. It isn't necessary to be ordained in order to be close to God.

Members of the laity are also called to holiness. By making me wait, the Lord opened my eyes to this. I now believe that he was never calling me to become a permanent deacon but was instead calling me to get to know him better.

The Lord knows me very well; he fully understands that I tend to be overzealous. Rather than let me jump headfirst into diaconate formation, he closed a few doors until I could learn something. Because I can be a bit dense, that lesson took a few years to learn. It was worth the wait!

Why Not Now?

God sometimes makes us wait for an answer. Sometimes it's hard to understand why he does that. I can think of a few good reasons.

Human Nature

One of the problems that many of us have is the tendency to forget about God once we get what we want. Although none of us like to admit this, it's a very common problem. We see numerous examples in the Old Testament. Time and time again, the Israelites would turn to the Lord when they were in trouble. When they got what they wanted, however, they abandoned God until the next crisis.

Let's face it, the Lord knows us better than we know ourselves. He is fully aware that if he grants all our requests, we may forget about him. Fortunately, he loves us too much to let that happen. He often delays in responding so that we can grow spiritually.

Once we begin praying for something, there's a very good chance that we'll continue to pray until we get what we want. As we continue to pray, what happens? We grow closer to the Lord because we're speaking to him frequently. Whether we're asking the Lord for a favor or trying to receive clear direction, the same principle applies. More communication equals better relationship. In the end, a better relationship with the Lord is well worth any waiting that we may have to endure.

Timing

Even though we may be in a hurry, sometimes the Lord knows that it's best to wait. He may be fully willing to give us what we want or provide the next piece of the puzzle, but the time might not be right.

When I decided that I wanted to work full-time for the Lord, I was ready to get started! Looking back, however, it's clear that God knew I wasn't ready. There were many things that I needed to learn before sharing my message with a large audience.

One of the most important concepts the Lord has taught me over the past few years is just how much I need him. As someone who tends to be controlling, my zeal to make things happen can easily allow me to forget that major concept. Although I'm still learning, I understand much more about God's role in my work than I did a few years ago.

When the time was right, he planted the desire to grow closer to him in my heart. A little while later, he gave me the desire to work for him on a full-time basis. Finally, when he thought I was ready, the Lord pulled the trigger, so to speak, and allowed me to get laid off and begin a career as a full-time evangelist. Once again, he knew best.

Growing Faith

It doesn't take faith to believe in something you can see. The Bible states that "faith is the assurance of things hoped for, the conviction of things not seen" (Hebrews 11:1). Jesus said, "Blessed are those who have not seen and yet believe" (John 20:29).

Most of us know how frustrating it can be when God is silent. That frustration can grow exponentially if we're trying to make a decision and the Lord seems to be on vacation. Even though we may not enjoy the experience, God sometimes remains silent so that our faith will grow. We are called to follow him even though we can't see the road ahead.

Abraham, Moses, Mary, Joseph, and Paul all knew what it was like to receive "Just trust me" as an answer to their prayers for clarity:

By faith Abraham obeyed when he was called to go out to a place which he was to receive as an inheritance; and he went out, not knowing where he was to go. (Hebrews 11:8)

By faith [Moses] left Egypt, not being afraid of the anger of the king; for he endured as seeing him who is invisible. (Hebrews 11:27)

Jesus said to them, 'How is it that you sought me? Did you not know that I must be in my Father's house?' And they did not understand the saying which he spoke to them. And he went down with them and came to Nazareth, and was obedient to them; and his mother kept all these things in her heart. (Luke 2:49–51)

Three times I besought the Lord about this, that it should leave me; but he said to me, "My grace is sufficient for you, for my power is made perfect in weakness." (2 Corinthians 12:8–9)

When God seems to not answer, it often means that he wants us to "walk by faith, not by sight" (2 Corinthians 5:7).

Lessons to Learn

Unlike many of us, the Lord is very patient. If he wants us to learn a lesson, he will find a way to make it happen. This may involve letting us flounder for a while. If we are serious about following him and continue to pray, we will eventually discover what he's trying to teach us.

As I wrote previously, I was miserable for the last few years that I worked as a project manager. I knew that the Lord wanted me to do something else with my life. After struggling for a long time, something hit me right between the eyes in the fall of 2011. I finally told Jesus that I was willing to stay at my current job if that's what he wanted me to do. I immediately felt an overwhelming sense of peace.

Shortly thereafter, I was laid off. While I can't say for sure, the sense of peace and the subsequent layoff seemed to indicate that the Lord had been waiting for me to surrender to his will, even if I didn't like it. Once I learned that lesson, I was able to move on to the next phase of his plan.

Attempting to discern God's will, especially when it comes to major decisions, can take a long time. And we can prolong the process if we aren't listening carefully. If we continue to seek his guidance, he will provide us with the information we need, when we need it. His timing is perfect.

> Wait for the Lord;
>> be strong, and let your heart take courage;
>> yes, wait for the Lord! (Psalm 27:14)

KEY POINTS
1. God is at work in our lives even when he appears to be silent.
2. When faced with a major decision, the discernment process can take months or even years.
3. Sometimes God will delay answering our prayer until our relationship with him grows stronger or until we learn an important lesson.
4. The lack of an answer from the Lord provides us with an opportunity to walk by faith.
5. If God wants us to know something, he will reveal it to us.

REFLECTION QUESTIONS
1. Do you get impatient when God doesn't answer right away?

2. Are you waiting on an answer from the Lord? What could he be trying to tell you? Have you asked him?

3. Have you ever stopped praying for something because God took too long to answer? Would you do the same thing today?

4. Have you asked the Lord to make you more patient?

5. Are you willing to accept God's current plan for your life, even if it involves suffering?

CHAPTER NINE

Decisions by the Book

WE HAVE ALREADY TOUCHED ON HOW SAMUEL, ELIJAH, AND MARY sought out and followed God's will. Through careful listening, they were able to hear the Lord's voice. More importantly, they responded to his call and made a conscious decision to obey his request.

The Bible contains many stories of individuals who were faced with similar decisions: Should I do what I want or what God wants? Not everyone decided to do things God's way. No matter how they responded, however, we can learn valuable lessons from their stories.

ADAM AND EVE

After creating Adam and placing him in the garden, the Lord gave him a very clear set of instructions. Adam was free to eat the fruit from every tree in the garden except "the tree of the knowledge of good and evil" (Genesis 2:17). Eating from the forbidden tree would result in death. We tend to look at Adam's case and see a no-brainer. The garden boasted "every tree that is pleasant to the sight and good for food" (Genesis 2:9). Why eat from the one forbidden tree?

Unfortunately, as we all know, the desires for pleasure and power can lead human beings to make wrong decisions. Adam and Eve were about to make a *very* poor decision!

In his desire to lure souls away from God, the evil one can be extremely creative. Appearing as a serpent in the Garden of Eden, he chose to approach Adam's wife and ask her a question: "Did God say, 'You shall not eat of any tree of the garden'?" (Genesis 3:1).

Judging from her answer, it was clear that Eve understood the command given to Adam by the Lord: "We may eat of the fruit of the trees of the garden; but God said, 'You shall not eat of the fruit of the tree which is in the midst of the garden, neither shall you touch it, lest you die'" (Genesis 3:2–3).

Undaunted by Eve's understanding of God's command, the serpent proceeded to do what he does best—he lied. And not only did he lie, but he lied in a big way. Completely contradicting God's instructions to Adam, the serpent assured Eve that eating the fruit would not cause her to die. He went on to plant seeds of doubt in her mind. He informed her that God didn't want her to eat the fruit because doing so would make her like God.

Amazing, isn't it? The enemy will stop at nothing in order to make us turn away from the Lord. And his methods are very effective!

Once Eve began to suspect God's motives, she turned her attention to the tree. Not only did it look good, but its fruit would allow her to become wise. She made her decision. She took the fruit, ate it, and gave some to Adam, who also ate. As a result of Adam and Eve's disobedience, death entered the world.

Let's not allow familiarity with this story to deaden its powerful message. There will be times in our lives when God wants us to do something that we don't want to do. Conversely, he may not want us to do something that we want to do. The devil loves these situations, and he'll try to convince us that it's OK. He may plant the idea that, even though the Church condemns a certain action, Jesus wouldn't agree.

Don't fall for the devil's lies! Although God ultimately brought good out of evil and sent us a Savior to repair the damage caused by Adam and Eve's disobedience, our first parents did not choose wisely. They made the wrong decision and paid the price.

Gideon

The Lord often speaks to us unexpectedly. We'll be performing our daily duties when suddenly ideas pop into our heads. Should I be doing something else with my life? Am I doing all I can to help the poor? Is there something I can do to help at my parish?

While we sometimes dismiss these thoughts, they are often God's ways of communicating with us. Gideon serves as a reminder that the Lord visits us in the midst of our ordinary duties and sometimes asks us to perform extraordinary tasks (see Judges 6:11–40).

Israel was under the constant threat of attack from the Midianites and Amalekites. These nomadic tribes were known for their practice of ravaging the land to obtain supplies. One day, as Gideon was beating out wheat in a wine press "to hide it from the Midianites," he was visited by an angel, who told him to "deliver Israel from the hand of Midian" (Judges 6:11–14).

Gideon responded in a way that will sound familiar to many of us: "Pray, Lord, how can I deliver Israel? Behold, my clan is the weakest in Manasseh, and I am the least in my family" (Judges 6:15). Essentially, Gideon told the Lord that he had picked the wrong guy!

How many of us respond that way when we are asked to lector at Mass, distribute Holy Communion, give to the poor? This response usually results from one of two reasons: Either we feel that it's not really God speaking to us, or we feel that we're incapable of carrying out the mission. While the former reason is justifiable and indicates a desire to discern God's will, the latter option is often rooted in pride.

We often forget that God doesn't expect us to do his work all by ourselves. He wants to help us! After the Lord patiently assured Gideon of his assistance (see Judges 6:16), the cautious man responded with a very wise request: "If now I have found favor with thee, then show me a sign that it is you who speak with me" (Judges 6:17).

Does this sound familiar? Gideon is responding to the Lord's call in the same way that many of us do. Our initial reaction is "I can't do this!" As we pray about the request and God assures us, usually with a feeling of peace, that he will help us, our next question is, "How do I know that it's really God who is asking me to do this?"

Although we may be hesitant to ask God for a sign, there's nothing wrong with doing so. If we're serious about doing what he wants, we should also be serious about verifying that the call is coming from him.

On the other hand, we must be willing to accept the fact that sometimes his answer will be "Trust me." The Lord knows what's best for each of us. In Gideon's case, God did indeed send a sign, along with words of assurance: "Peace be to you; do not fear, you shall not die" (Judges 6:23).

Despite the fact that he was afraid, Gideon followed the Lord's instructions to destroy his father's altar dedicated to the false god Baal and replace it with an altar to the true God. As promised, Gideon was not harmed after performing this bold action. By giving him this initial mission, the Lord built Gideon's faith in preparation for his ultimate task: freeing Israel from the threat of the Midianites.

When preparing for this mission, Gideon once again asked for a sign:

> If thou wilt deliver Israel by my hand, as thou hast said, behold, I am laying a fleece of wool on the threshing floor; if there is dew on the fleece alone, and it is dry on all the ground, then I shall know that thou wilt deliver Israel by my hand, as thou hast said. (Judges 6:36–37)

The Lord provided the sign. Then Gideon had the audacity to ask for the opposite sign:

> "Let not thy anger burn against me, let me speak but this once; pray, let me make trial only this once with the fleece; pray, let

it be dry only on the fleece, and on all the ground let there be dew." And God did so that night; for it was dry on the fleece only, and on all the ground there was dew. (Judges 6:39–40)

Gideon was finally convinced. Now the Lord, to ensure that the people realized that he alone was their deliverer, instructed Gideon to drastically reduce the size of his army. Gideon did as he was instructed, without asking for any additional signs, and his army easily defeated the Midianites (see Judges 7:2–22)

Although he was afraid and hesitant, Gideon tried his best to follow God's will. He listened for the Lord's voice and asked questions when things were unclear. Most importantly, however, he trusted. As a result, God used him to accomplish a great task.

No matter how diligent we are when attempting to make decisions that please the Lord, some element of faith is always necessary. God is good for his word. It is always wise to trust him.

Samuel

While we have previously looked at Samuel's struggle to hear God's voice (see chapter 7), there's another episode in his life that warrants a close look. You'll see from this story that sometimes God gives us an answer that we don't want to hear. How we respond in such cases speaks volumes about our desire to follow him. Are we prepared to obey the Lord even if it's not what we want?

In an effort to be like the surrounding nations, the Israelites wanted a king. When they approached Samuel and requested that he appoint a king, he was not pleased with the idea (see 1 Samuel 8:5–6). Instead of simply refusing, however, Samuel prayed to the Lord. Even though he already had an opinion, Samuel didn't want to choose without letting God weigh in.

As he sometimes does, God answered in a surprising manner: "Hearken to the voice of the people in all that they say to you; for they have not rejected you, but they have rejected me from being king over them" (1 Samuel 8:7). The Lord also told Samuel to warn the Israelites of the dangers that awaited them under their desired king.

Despite the ugly picture Samuel presented (verses 10–18), the people persisted in their demand for a king. Still uncomfortable with the idea, Samuel turned once again to the Lord and informed him of their decision. God responded: "Hearken to their voice, and make them a king" (1 Samuel 8:22).

Samuel went along with the Lord's plan. Shortly thereafter, Saul was chosen as the first king of Israel (see 1 Samuel 10:1). Because of his disobedience, however, Saul was eventually rejected by the Lord (see 1 Samuel 15:10–11), and David was chosen as his replacement.

When we look at this story with 20/20 hindsight and from a purely human point of view, it's easy to question God's logic. Why did he choose a king who would prove to be disobedient? Why did Israel need a king at all? It almost appears as if Samuel knew more than God.

Samuel presents a powerful lesson for those of us who are trying to make decisions that please the Lord. God always knows best, and he brings good even out of evil. Let's remember this in the daily choices we face.

The Rich Young Man

Asking questions is a very important step in the process of acquiring knowledge. And one of the most important questions that we can ask is: "What must I do to get to heaven?" If we sincerely pose this to the Lord, we will get an answer. Unfortunately, that answer may not be one that we want to hear. That's exactly what happened to the rich young man in Matthew 19:16–22.

DECISIONS BY THE BOOK

The encounter between Jesus and the rich man started off on a very positive note: "Teacher, what good deed must I do, to have eternal life?" (Matthew 19:16).

If this question was coming from a sincere heart, it would indicate that the man was trying to follow the Lord to the best of his ability. After all, someone who didn't care about following Jesus or getting to heaven wouldn't be asking such a question. The Lord's response to "keep the commandments" hardly came as a surprise.

In an apparent attempt to come to a deeper understanding of Jesus's response, the young man asked for more specifics. While it's impossible to know for sure, it certainly seems that the man's curiosity was sincere. After being reminded of the commandments by the Lord, the young man was still not satisfied: "All these I have observed; what do I still lack?" (Matthew 19:20).

I have to be honest when I tell you that I don't think I would have asked that last question. To his credit, however, this young man kept pushing for answers. At this point, it seems as if he would be an excellent role model for those of us who are trying to follow God's will. Not only did the young man obey the commandments, but he approached the Lord and asked what more he needed to do to get to heaven. Sounds as if he was following all the right steps for discerning God's will, doesn't it?

Unfortunately, the man was about to receive an answer that didn't please him: "If you would be perfect, go, sell what you possess and give to the poor, and you will have treasure in heaven; and come, follow me" (Matthew 19:21).

The Lord's answer proved too much for the rich young man, and "he went away sorrowful; for he had great possessions" (Matthew 19:22). Sad, isn't it? He had no problem keeping the commandments and asked many questions about how he could become holier, but he wasn't willing to part with his possessions. Obviously, he loved his possessions more than he loved the Lord.

While it's true that this story doesn't have a happy ending (at least as far as we know), we can learn a lot by looking at the rich young man. Even though he made the wrong decision in the end, he also did several things right.

First of all, we have to admire him for keeping the commandments. That's a given for anyone who's serious about following God's will. Second, he thought about getting to heaven. That's a good thing too. He then took it to the next level and asked Jesus for advice about becoming holy. Furthermore, he listened to the Lord's responses and asked follow-up questions.

These are all important steps when trying to determine what God wants us to do. In the end, however, the young man wasn't willing to obey the Lord's instruction. His material possessions were more important than following Jesus and getting to heaven. When it comes to bad decisions, it doesn't get much worse than this!

St. Joseph

While the Bible tells us very little about the life of St. Joseph, we can learn what we need to know. He was "a just man" (Matthew 1:19), wanting to do what was right in the eyes of God. Because of this goodness, Joseph reacted in an unusual way when he learned that Mary was pregnant. In order to spare her any embarrassment, he decided to quietly end their betrothal (their marriage was already considered to be legally binding and could only be terminated by death or divorce). While his plan may sound strange to us, it would have protected Mary from being condemned.

Joseph thought he was making a just and good decision, but the Lord had something better in mind. And as the Lord often does when he wants to send a message, he intervened and provided Joseph with a new plan. He sent an angel to Joseph in a dream, and he delivered the following message:

> Joseph, son of David, do not fear to take Mary your wife, for that which is conceived in her is of the Holy Spirit; she will bear a son, and you shall call his name Jesus, for he will save his people from their sins. (Matthew 1:20–21)

Despite the fact that the message seemed far-fetched, Joseph recognized the Lord speaking to him through the angel. He put aside his initial plan to divorce Mary and "did as the angel of the Lord commanded him" (Matthew 1:24). Even though his initial choice would have been honorable, Joseph surrendered to God's will and obeyed the angel's instructions. That flexibility and the desire to do what God wanted were characteristic of St. Joseph. As a result, he is an excellent role model for all decision makers.

The Best Option

Sacred Scripture is filled with stories of people who had major decisions to make. Some made poor choices (Rehoboam in 1 Kings 12:1–15), some resisted at first but eventually acquiesced (Naaman in 2 Kings 5:1–14), and some responded to God's voice with prompt obedience (Paul in Acts 9:1–19). As we strive to follow God's will, it would be wise to let him speak to us through the lives of these individuals.

How about us? Are we truly seeking to make decisions that will please the Lord? Are we attempting to hear his voice? Do we obey his instructions?

One thing never changes: We can choose to please God, or we can choose to please ourselves. The first option works out much better in the long run!

KEY POINTS

1. Satan will stop at nothing to get us to turn away from the Lord. He lies to us in an attempt to lead us to decisions that will not please God.

2. Adam and Eve understood God's will but chose to pursue pleasure and power instead.

3. As illustrated by Gideon, it's a good idea to ask questions if we're not sure of what God wants us to do.

4. Sometimes God will ask us to do something that we would rather not do. This is a great opportunity to show our love for him.

5. St. Joseph was open to God's will even when it involved doing something very difficult. He provides us with a great example.

REFLECTION QUESTIONS

1. Do you typically consult God when making major decisions?

2. Does your desire to please the Lord outweigh your personal desires?

3. Are you open to whatever God asks you to do, or are some options out of the question?

4. Given that his original plan appeared logical, why do you think Joseph was able to follow the angel's unconventional advice?

5. Can you relate to the rich young man's dilemma? Have you ever made a similar decision?

Chapter Ten

Jump In!

At this point, I'm sure that you're well aware that God cares about what you do in your life. In fact, holiness, to which we're all called, is simply a matter of doing God's will. You may have to work at it a bit, but if God is calling you to do something, you're probably going to know it. The Lord isn't going to speak to you using undecipherable language. When you get a feeling that you should do something (or not do something), you should take the appropriate steps to determine if that feeling is coming from the Lord. Once you determine to the best of your ability that your potential choice is what the Lord wants, there's only one thing left to do. It's the same thing that you do when you see a swimming pool on a hot day—jump in!

Just as you can never be sure what the water will feel like until you dive into the pool, you can never be certain what will happen when you put your proposed action into practice. There's simply no getting around it. Although it gets easier as our faith grows stronger, sometimes responding to God's call can be frightening. This is especially true when it involves an unfamiliar situation or an uncertain path. We can be sure of one thing, however. If we're sincerely trying to do God's will, there is no way that he will abandon us.

One thing to keep in mind as you try to discern God's will is that things will usually look and feel different on paper (or in your thoughts) than in real life. Way back in driver's education class, I learned how to react to a patch of ice on the street. My book knowledge only got me so far when my car actually skidded on ice.

In the same way, a carefully thought out plan may experience a few glitches when executed. Don't panic. Once you make a decision that's based upon pleasing God, you should act on it even if you're not 100 percent certain you can handle it. He will be with you!

SCHOOL BELLES

Just after our twins were born, Eileen and I were given a flyer about Catholic homeschooling. We looked through it and got a good feeling. We both agreed that it would be a nice idea and even signed up for the sponsor's mailing list. As first-time parents with premature twins, there is no way that we could have anticipated some of the issues we would soon be facing.

The first lesson we learned is that being a parent is a lot more difficult than we thought it would be. As a result, when the homeschooling flyer came in the mail the next year, we chuckled a bit and deposited it in the trash. As the years progressed and the girls become more active, the annual flyer became a source of greater amusement for us. Our typical response when it came in the mail was something to the effect of "Yeah, right!" In other words, homeschooling was no longer a serious option for us.

We eventually enrolled Mary and Elizabeth in the local public school, where they did reasonably well. They had some learning disabilities due to their prematurity but nothing that couldn't be handled.

As the years passed, we became concerned about some of the things taking place in the school. Reservations about what was being taught plus some bullying incidents caused us to revisit the homeschooling idea. We prayed about it, discussed it with other homeschooling parents, and surprisingly, were increasingly drawn to the idea. What we had previously considered impossible became a viable option.

Yet, we were still a bit skeptical. In April 2011, we decided to attend one of the homeschooling conferences that we had been hearing about since the girls were newborns. As we listened to the speakers and spoke with the vendors, the call to take the plunge increased. At the end of the day, Eileen and I both agreed that we should do the unthinkable. We were sure that God was calling us to enter the world of homeschooling.

We were uncertain how the girls would react. They were in the sixth grade, and this would be a big change for them. We informed Mary and Elizabeth as soon as we got home, and we were thrilled to discover that they liked the idea. This just about sealed the deal for us. Barring any unforeseen circumstances, the Zimak family was about to become a homeschooling family!

Not everyone approved of the idea. This was a bit disappointing, but we weren't totally surprised. You might have the greatest idea in the world, and it could be exactly in line with God's will, but you are always going to have people who tell you it's a bad idea. Let's face it, people even laughed at Jesus when he was about to restore a girl to life (see Mark 5:39–40).

One of the key things to remember is that not all opinions are created equal. Learning to listen to the right people is critical when making decisions.

We continued to pray and definitely felt that the Lord was calling us to become homeschooling parents. We selected a Catholic curriculum provider, purchased supplies, and selected the location for our classroom (the dining room). We even bought a bell to ring at the beginning of the school day!

Eileen got a little anxious when the box of books arrived. I had two fears in the back of my mind—that I would lose my job and that Eileen would get seriously ill—but I dismissed them as irrational. As the school year approached, we experienced a mix of butterflies and excitement. Deep in our hearts, however, we knew that it would work out because it was God's will.

As I was leaving for work on the first day of school, I observed a heartwarming vision in the dining room. Eileen and the girls were gathered around the table, ready to begin. The smiles on their faces reassured me that we had made the correct decision. I kissed them good-bye, anxious to hear how the big day would go.

As I sat in my office that day, I kept picturing the scene at the dining room table. I didn't want to disturb the school day, so I vowed to wait until lunch before phoning home. When I finally made the call, Eileen answered, and I asked how it was going. I was totally unprepared for what I was about to hear. "It's horrible!" she sobbed. "We all hate it!"

Before I could ask another question, Eileen asked one of her own. "Why would God trick us like this?" At this point, I have to admit that I was at a loss for words. We had spent months carefully discerning this decision. How could we have made the wrong choice?

While my initial reaction was to panic and start thinking about a list of potential Catholic elementary schools for the girls, I eventually calmed down and began to pray. When I arrived home, Eileen and I discussed the situation, recalling how much prayer and research had gone into this decision. We decided to give it more time. After all, one day is hardly long enough to validate an important decision.

Eventually, things calmed down, and everyone settled into a routine. Although it can be challenging at times, homeschooling has been a great experience for us and has brought us closer together as a family. The girls are now in high school, and we continue to homeschool. We fully believe that the Lord is calling us to do this, though it sure didn't seem like it on the first day.

Always give your decision some time. Bumps in the road don't necessarily indicate that the decision was wrong. Often, the difficulties are just God's way of helping you to trust him more. Just look at St. Peter.

ON TROUBLED WATERS

Peter and the other apostles knew something about water. Several of them were fishermen by trade and were used to being on the sea. One night, as they were in a boat being battered by the sea and wind, Jesus appeared to them (see Matthew 14:25). He was walking on the water.

One doesn't need to be a fisherman to know that walking on water is not ordinarily possible. Understandably, the apostles were afraid. They thought they might be seeing a ghost. Jesus urged the men to have no fear. And then Peter spoke up:

> "Lord, if it is you, bid me come to you on the water." [Jesus] said, "Come." So Peter got out of the boat and walked on the water and came to Jesus; but when he saw the wind, he was afraid, and beginning to sink he cried out, "Lord, save me." Jesus immediately reached out his hand and caught him, saying to him, "O you of little faith, why did you doubt?" (Matthew 14:28–31)

When Peter first saw Jesus walking on the water, he wondered if it was really the Lord, and then proceeded to do something very logical: He asked for a sign. When Jesus instructed him, "Come," Peter obeyed. He stepped out of the boat, taking a big risk. He literally put his life in the Lord's hands.

If this happened to you, would you step out of the boat onto the turbulent sea? I have to be honest and tell you that I'm not so sure that I would. I have my limits when it comes to trusting the Lord. I don't have a problem trusting him with small matters; it's the big things that make me waver.

I see some similarities between Peter's leap into the water and our first attempts to homeschool. Prior to putting the plan into action, our eyes were on Jesus. Like Peter, Eileen and I heard the Lord calling us to do something. After making sure that the call was coming from him, we went for it. Our supposedly good idea became a lot more frightening once we tried to put it into practice. Like Peter on the water, we became overwhelmed by the details and took our eyes off of Jesus. And just like Peter, we began to sink.

If the Lord is calling us to do something, he won't abandon us. It's extremely important to rely on him not only when we are coming to a decision but also as we are carrying out our planned action. When Jesus said, "I am with you always" (Matthew 28:20), he wasn't kidding!

What If I'm Wrong?

All of this is great, you might think, provided that we are doing what God wants. But what happens when the unthinkable occurs? What can we do if we make the wrong decision and choose something that God doesn't want for us? Will he desert us because we didn't listen?

I have to admit that it is possible for a sincere Christian to make a wrong choice. The methods in this book will increase your chances for choosing in accordance with God's will, but they are no guarantee. Now that we have the bad news out of the way, let's discuss the good news.

God remains faithful:

> I will instruct you and teach you
> the way you should go;
> I will counsel you with my eye upon you. (Psalm 32:8)

In the event that you unknowingly choose the wrong option, God will not abandon you. If you care about doing his will, he is going to be very pleased with you. Even if you make a mistake, he'll find a way to draw good from it or to give you another chance.

Need some proof? Let's look at another example from the life of St. Peter. When it comes to bad decisions, he made one of the worst. Despite a serious lack of judgment on his part, however, the Lord gave him another chance.

After promising Jesus that he was ready to go to prison and even die with him, Peter went on to deny the Lord—not once but three times (see Luke 22:33, 54–62)! The head of the apostles was very human and had some well-publicized character flaws. There's no doubt he made a bad decision, correct? In fact, chances are very good that you and I aren't going to make one that bad, especially if we're trying to carefully discern God's will.

Following Peter's bad decision, however, Jesus was willing to give him another chance. After Jesus had risen from the dead, he appeared to the apostles while they were out fishing. After they came ashore, Jesus asked Peter three times if he loved him (see John 21:15–17). Peter answered that he did.

That's three denials next to a charcoal fire, followed by three chances for redemption, also next to a charcoal fire. Coincidence? Hardly! Peter's big bloopers and his subsequent declarations of love for the Lord have inspired and guided Christians through the centuries. Let them give you hope.

Don't worry about making a bad decision. Once you determine that the Lord is calling you to do something, go ahead and do it. No matter what happens, God can always bring good out of it.

KEY POINTS

1. If God wants you to do something, he will let you know.

2. Once you've carefully determined that God is calling you to do something, you should take action and do it.

3. The fact that difficulties may arise with your plan doesn't mean that it isn't God's will. He often allows us to struggle in order to increase our faith.

4. Although the chances decrease as your prayer and discernment increase, it's still possible to make the wrong choice.

5. Even if you make the wrong choice, take comfort in the fact that the Lord will help you get back on the right track. He can bring good out of any situation.

REFLECTION QUESTIONS

1. Have you ever failed to act on something you felt God was calling you to do? What stopped you?

2. Are you afraid to act on your decisions, even if you think they're what the Lord wants?

3. Is there something you feel God may be calling you to do? What's the worst that could happen if you're wrong?

4. Have you ever made a poor choice about something? What happened? Did any good come out of it?

5. Did you ever make a mistake and have a chance to redeem yourself? How often has this happened?

Chapter Eleven

Peace

The peace of God, which passes all understanding, will keep your minds and your hearts in Christ Jesus.

—Philippians 4:7

JUST AS WE SHOULD ASK GOD TO HELP US MAKE CORRECT DECISIONS, we should also ask him to confirm our choices. The ordinary way that the Lord reveals that we are doing what he wants us to do is by giving us a sense of peace. It's his way of letting us know that we're on the right track. Just ask yourself, "Am I peaceful?" While that peace can be felt throughout the day, it should be especially strong when you pray.

Now, the absence of peace doesn't necessarily mean that you made a wrong choice. Restlessness in our spirits can have many causes. We'll look at some of these too in this chapter.

A LIFE-AND-DEATH DECISION

Before they were born, our twins suffered from a very serious medical condition known as twin-to-twin transfusion syndrome. Diagnosed in the eighteenth week of Eileen's pregnancy, this extremely serious medical condition put the lives of Mary and Elizabeth in jeopardy. In fact, their odds for survival were not good.

Immediately upon receiving the news, we began to pray and asked for prayers from everyone we knew. We also pursued the recommended medical treatment. Twice each week, an ultrasound was performed, and the girls' hearts were checked. The main reason for the ultrasound was to see if the girls were still alive.

Almost immediately, Elizabeth developed congestive heart failure. This condition was just about impossible to treat in utero. We were informed that if Elizabeth succumbed to the heart failure, it was very likely that Mary would die from the associated shock to her system.

We experienced many ups and downs over the course of the next few months. Some days we received good news, and other days the news was grim. Although the doctors tried a few experimental treatments, there wasn't much they could do. Eileen and I took one day at a time, leaning heavily on those who supported us through prayer.

One day, we received some especially bad news from one of the doctors. After looking at the ultrasound and echocardiogram results, he informed us that Elizabeth would probably die within the next week or two. It was still very early in the pregnancy, and delivering the girls at that time was not a realistic option. The only other thing we could try, according to the doctor, was an experimental surgery that was performed by a major hospital across the river in Philadelphia. He gave us the phone number of the specialist who performed this surgery and recommended that we call for more information.

Eileen and I were stunned as we discussed the pros and cons of pursuing this path. There was something about this course of action that didn't seem right. But we decided that it couldn't hurt to call for some information.

After a weekend of praying and talking it over with family members, I made the phone call on Monday. I was not prepared for the receptionist's question. Was I calling about a selective reduction or laser surgery?

I don't have a medical background, but I knew what "selective reduction" is. It is a euphemism for the abortion of one or more multiples.

Although the receptionist's question sent me reeling, I managed to ask one or two prepared questions about the laser surgery. The receptionist told me that the doctor would call back.

Even though this appeared to be the only hope of saving the girls, Eileen and I couldn't get past the fact that the surgeon who would perform the operation also performed abortions. We prayed and asked family members for advice and prayers. By the time the doctor called back, we had already reached a tentative decision not to go with the surgery. The information he provided confirmed our choice. He had only done a few of these surgeries, and the results were unimpressive.

Still, Eileen and I were plagued by the thought that we might be acting irresponsibly. Were we doing all we could to protect the lives of our children? What would the doctors say? What would our family and friends say? Maybe we were too close to the situation and weren't being as objective as we should be. Yet, continued prayer brought us peace.

In the days that followed, confirmation came from some surprising sources. A neighbor commented, "Doctors don't always have all the answers, and sometimes you just have to trust God." A family member advised, "It's better to have them die by the hand of God than by the hand of a surgeon." These unexpected comments brought us a sense of comfort. Yet, nothing was as comforting as the message that we received when we returned to our doctor's office later that week.

A team of specialists was handling the girls' case, and the doctor we consulted that day was one we hadn't seen in several weeks. When we told him that we were not going to pursue surgery, we both felt a weight lifting from our shoulders. Even though we weren't aware of any other options, we felt very peaceful.

Much to our surprise, the doctor was fine with our decision. Our peace grew as he offered the option of heart medication for Eileen in the hope that it would find its way to Elizabeth's heart. He also mentioned injections that would help the girls' lungs develop faster, thus improving the chances for survival if they were born prematurely. Our feeling of peace grew. Even if the girls didn't survive, we knew that we were doing the right thing.

Mary and Elizabeth entered the world three months early on October 27, 1997. Despite many bumps in the road, they are now healthy teenagers. They are living examples of Gabriel's words, "With God nothing will be impossible" (Luke 1:37)!

MISSING PEACE

Peace is definitely a byproduct of doing God's will. No matter how many challenges you encounter in life, staying close to the Lord will allow your heart to be filled with peace. How important is peace? After he rose from the dead, Jesus's first words to his frightened and discouraged apostles were "Peace be with you" (John 20:21).

Unfortunately, sometimes the chaos of our daily lives can drown out that peace. Your best chance of regaining it is to pray. After making a decision, spend some time with Jesus in the Blessed Sacrament, at an adoration chapel or in a church where the Blessed Sacrament is in the tabernacle. Allow yourself some time to relax, clear your mind from the distractions of daily life, and rest in the presence of the Lord. When you feel ready, ask him this simple question: "Did I do what you wanted, Lord?"

Trust me, he will let you know. The Lord's presence is the perfect place to hear his voice, and the Lord wants us to hear him. He desires that we understand his will for our lives. Just as little children seek the approval of their parents, we should similarly seek the Lord's approval.

What if you don't feel peace? Does that mean you made a bad decision or are not following God's will? Maybe, maybe not. Let's explore some reasons for a lack of peace in our lives.

Have I Offended the Lord?

The Lord will let us know when our actions are not pleasing to him. While it may not be pleasant to receive this news from him, it can be a blessing. If we are doing something that doesn't please the Lord, isn't it better to know about it while we still have time to make changes? Whether you made a bad decision, committed a serious sin, or are simply neglecting your relationship with God, it's not too late to make amends. There have been many occasions when my guilty conscience let me know that I was on the wrong track, and I am grateful!

It's always a good idea to investigate the cause of your unease. When in doubt, a thorough examination of conscience is a good place to start. (See chapter 4 for a refresher on that.)

Desolations

Is it possible for us to lack peace even if we are doing what the Lord wants? Technically, yes. Remember the discussion of consolations and desolations in chapter six. Sometimes the Lord allows us to experience periods of desolation—dryness or negativity. While they can be unpleasant, desolation can actually strengthen our faith, and that's why God permits it.

As a general rule, if your lack of peace is persistent, it's likely that you are doing something that doesn't please God. If it comes and goes, there is a good chance that it's being caused by desolations. Keep pursuing God.

Part of a Bigger Plan

There is another reason why you may not experience peace even after making a decision that pleases the Lord. Sometimes your initial choice is the first part of a bigger plan, and God now wants you to move on to the next step.

When Elijah was first called to be a prophet, the Lord gave him the following instructions:

Depart from here and turn eastward, and hide yourself by the
brook Cherith, that is east of the Jordan. You shall drink from
the brook, and I have commanded the ravens to feed you there.
(1 Kings 17:3–4)

Elijah obeyed the Lord. As the Lord had promised, the ravens fed him,
and he drank from the brook. After a while, however, the brook dried
up because of a severe drought (see 1 Kings 17:7).

If I were in Elijah's shoes, the lack of drinking water would have
certainly gotten my attention. I'd be turning to the Lord for help. I
suppose that's what Elijah did. Guess what happened? The Lord gave
the prophet instructions to go to Zarephath, where he would be fed by
a widow (see 1 Kings 17:9).

Why didn't God just send Elijah directly to Zarephath without
asking him to first live by the brook? Possibly because he wanted to
teach Elijah about his providence before sending him on a greater
mission. God often calls us to do something for a short period of time
before giving us another task. The lack of peace along the way may indicate that he's got something else in mind for us.

Remember this: The Lord wants us to be at peace, and the closer we
are to him, the more peace we will feel. Peace is a good indicator that
our actions are pleasing to him. On the other hand, a persistent lack of
peace typically indicates that the Lord is trying to get your attention.
Give him that attention, and he will show you what's up!

And let the peace of Christ rule in your hearts, to which indeed
you were called in the one body. (Colossians 3:15)

Key Points

1. The best indicator that we have made the correct decision in God's
   eyes is a strong sense of peace.

2. While it's not proof positive that we are not doing God's will, the absence of peace in our lives always warrants a close look.
3. The best way to feel the Lord's peace (or lack thereof) is to pray in his presence.
4. Lack of peace can be caused by desolations, a normal part of the spiritual life.
5. Lack of peace can be God's way of letting us know that he has something else he'd like us to do.

REFLECTION QUESTIONS
1. Have you ever made a big decision and felt peaceful afterward? Have you ever experienced a lack of peace?
2. Are you peaceful at the moment? If not, have you asked the Lord why not?
3. After making a major decision, do you present it to Jesus for his approval?
4. Have you felt the Lord's peace even in the midst of suffering?
5. Why do you think that the first thing the risen Jesus did when he appeared to his apostles was to wish them peace?

CHAPTER TWELVE

Thy Will Be Done

DISCOVERING GOD'S WILL IS NOT AN EXACT SCIENCE—WITH ONE exception. There is a time when you can be positive that you are following the Lord's will. Unfortunately, it gets overlooked more often than not.

Fr. Lawrence Gesy's book *The Hem of His Garment*, which contains stories of miraculous healings, gave me great hope when my twin daughters were in utero. He made a statement that hit me like a ton of bricks and remains etched in my mind to this day: "A sign that God is working in your life is that he will lead you where you do not intend to go."[10]

Sometimes we are thrown into a completely unexpected situation. While it doesn't have to be an unpleasant one, it often is. A sudden illness, job layoff, relationship problem, or death in the family can cause us to panic and question God's providence.

Yet, there's something very positive taking place in these situations. Since they are completely out of our control, we can be sure that they represent God's will. The moment we find ourselves dealing with an event that is not of our choosing, *we are following God's will*. According to St. Alphonsus Liguori, "We must not…consider the afflictions that come upon us as happening by chance or solely from the malice of men; we should be convinced that what happens, happens by the will of God."[11]

Despite the fact that we may be following God's will, however, these unexpected situations can easily rob us of our peace. Why? It generally happens because our will and the Lord's will don't match up. In other words, sometimes what God wants isn't what we want.

While we won't experience any loss of peace if we truly believe the words we pray in the Lord's Prayer ("Thy will be done"), most of us need some improvement in that area. We lose our peace when something unpleasant happens in our life. Depending on the severity of the event, this loss of peace can become crippling and even plunge us into despair.

Jesus assures us that it is possible to experience peace even in the midst of great turmoil, as long as we remain close to him. "I have said this to you, that in me you may have peace. In the world you have tribulation; but be of good cheer, I have overcome the world" (John 16:33).

It is critical to the Christian life to accept the fact that whatever happens in your life is God's will. It's half the battle. The other half is learning to embrace suffering and uncomfortable situations as they arise. Let's look at some ways to put this into practice.

WHERE AM I?

Are you familiar with the phrase, "Bloom where you're planted"? It's a great reminder that God surrounds us with certain people and places us in certain situations for a reason. The Lord has given each of us unique gifts, or charisms. According to St. Paul, they are not given to us solely for personal use but rather to build up God's kingdom.

> Now there are varieties of gifts, but the same Spirit; and there are varieties of service, but the same Lord; and there are varieties of working, but it is the same God who inspires them all in every one. To each is given the manifestation of the Spirit for the common good. (1 Corinthians 12:4–7)

Some individuals are great speakers, others are great writers, some are skilled listeners, and others are good at working with the elderly. The Holy Spirit can work in different ways through different people. And that's a very good thing!

God surrounds us with people and situations that will allow us to do the greatest good. He knows which speakers and authors will appeal to us and which ones will leave us flat. He knows our strengths and weaknesses better than we know them. While we may not always enjoy where the Lord places us, he has us there for a reason.

Unfortunately, our unhappiness with various situations can cause us to waste opportunities. God promised that he will never give us more than we can handle (1 Corinthians 10:13), but a sudden crisis has a way of convincing us otherwise. We sometimes focus so much on the problem that we lose sight of everything else.

When faced with a painful cross that is not of your choosing, you have a choice to make. You have the option of rejecting your God-given cross by complaining or falling victim to self-pity. On the other hand, you have a great opportunity to put yourself at the service of the Lord and to actively follow his will.

When my mother-in-law was diagnosed with leukemia in May 2010, it came as a shock to her and to our entire family. She had always been relatively healthy and took good care of herself. A lack of energy and some serious bruising caused her to go to the doctor for testing, resulting in the grim diagnosis. Even though Betty had a strong faith, she was very frightened when she heard the news.

Betty had always sought to help others, and her suffering didn't stop that. One day, I had the privilege of accompanying her to the doctor's office for some blood work. Despite being very weak and not feeling well, Betty was incredibly nice to everyone at the office. She asked how they were doing, inquired about their plans for the weekend, and asked questions regarding previous conversations with them. Even though she was feeling lousy and was understandably concerned about her condition, Betty allowed herself to be the Lord's instrument and brought a great deal of joy to those around her.

As the illness and the treatments took a greater toll on her, Betty refused to give in to self-pity and continued to reach out to others. My wife witnessed one of the best examples of this when she took her mother for a platelet transfusion.

Because it was a lengthy procedure and required several hours at the hospital, Eileen went to look for something for her mother to eat. When she brought back a chocolate chip muffin from a snack bar in the lobby, a nurse commented on how tasty it looked. Several hours later, the transfusion was finished, and Eileen helped her weakened mother walk to the lobby and settle into a chair before getting the car. Betty saw that there was one chocolate chip muffin remaining in the snack bar's display. She gave Eileen money and asked her to buy it and take it to the nurse.

Even though we may not have a choice in some of the events that happen to us, we always have the opportunity to embrace God's will. It all begins with one simple question: Lord, how can I best serve you in this situation? It doesn't matter if we're in a doctor's waiting room, an unemployment office, or a hospital cafeteria. God places us where he needs us to be, even if we would rather be elsewhere. Learning to embrace his plan is not only the secret to peace but a guaranteed way to follow his will.

REDEMPTIVE SUFFERING

When I attended Catholic school in the sixties and seventies, I heard a lot about offering up suffering. Anytime something unpleasant happened, we were instructed to offer it up. It wasn't until many years later that I finally understood that this was more than just a saying.

When we offer up our suffering and unite it with the Lord's, we are actually assisting him with the redemption of the world. This is a tremendous honor and a great gift. Anytime anything unpleasant happens in our lives, we have the ability to climb up on the cross with Jesus and transform the pain into a powerful sacrifice. While suffering, in and of itself, has no intrinsic value, it takes on infinite value when offered to the Lord.

St. Paul experienced the benefit of offering his suffering to the Lord: "Now I rejoice in my sufferings for your sake, and in my flesh I complete what is lacking in Christ's afflictions for the sake of his body, that is, the church" (Colossians 1:24).

Yes, it is possible to be joyful in the midst of suffering. That joy doesn't come from the suffering itself but rather from the grace associated with doing the will of the Lord. Paul rejoiced not because of his suffering but because he was helping Jesus with his mission of redemption. And when it came to suffering, St. Paul certainly had his share. The verse above was composed while the apostle was in prison (see Colossians 4:3). If Paul could rejoice while he was under arrest, then it's possible for us to experience that same joy in whatever we are suffering. I find that to be very comforting, don't you?

There is no doubt that Jesus's life was about doing the will of his Father. He stated that he came from heaven "not to do my own will, but the will of him who sent me" (John 6:38). St. Paul writes that Christ "became obedient unto death, even death on a cross" (Philippians 2:8).

Because he was human (as well as divine), Jesus was able to suffer and even experience fear. While he could have suppressed these feelings of his human nature, he chose not to do so. As a result, he gave us a genuine example of what it means to submit to the Father's will, even in the face of dread. On the night before he died, Jesus knelt in prayer: "Father, if thou art willing, remove this cup from me; nevertheless not my will, but thine, be done" (Luke 22:42).

What a great prayer! Although he harbors the typical human aversion to suffering, Jesus surrenders his personal feelings and submits to the will of his Father. There can be no better example for us to follow.

When faced with unexpected suffering, we have a golden opportunity to express our love for the Lord by accepting his will. While it's true that we can embrace God's will even when he provides us with blue skies, our expression of love is magnified when we are in the midst of suffering: "This is painful, Lord, but I want what you want. I know that this is your will for me at the moment, and that's good enough for me."

Lessons from Job

When we think of suffering, the Old Testament hero Job often comes to mind. It would be quite an understatement to say that he didn't have it easy. If you're having a bad day, reading the first chapter of the book of Job should be enough to make you feel better!

The chapter introduces us to Job, a good man with a wife, seven sons, three daughters, several thousand animals, and many servants. Believing that Job would curse God if his good fortune was taken away, Satan received permission to test him. In one day, Job's servants were slaughtered, his animals were stolen, and his children were killed when their house collapsed on them.

Job's response was astonishing: "Naked I came from my mother's womb, and naked shall I return; the Lord gave, and the Lord has taken away; blessed be the name of the Lord" (Job 1:21). These are the words of a righteous man who is willing to accept God's will in all things.

Still hoping that Job would crack and turn against the Lord, Satan came up with another plan. Job was afflicted "with loathsome sores from the sole of his foot to the crown of his head" (Job 2:7). Job once again refused to curse the Lord. "Shall we receive good at the hand of God, and shall we not receive evil?" he asked (Job 2:10).

Eventually, Job started demanding answers. In the end, the Lord reminded him that some things are beyond human understanding:

> Shall a faultfinder contend with the Almighty?
> He who argues with God, let him answer it. (Job 40:2)

Job repented, and God more than restored his fortune.

> The Lord blessed the latter days of Job more than his beginning; and he had fourteen thousand sheep, six thousand camels, a thousand yoke of oxen, and a thousand she-donkeys. He had also seven sons and three daughters…. And in all the land there were no women so fair as Job's daughters; and their father gave them inheritance among their brothers. And after this Job lived a hundred and forty years, and saw his sons, and his sons' sons, four generations. (Job 42:12–13, 15–16)

There will be unpleasant, even tragic, events in our lives, many of which will be beyond our understanding. These situations provide us with great opportunities to trust in the Lord's providence and embrace his will for our lives.

As Jesus demonstrated, however, it's perfectly acceptable to ask God to remove our sufferings. Until that happens (or if it doesn't happen), we have the chance to embrace our cross. Whenever we do that, we can be absolutely certain that we are doing God's will. That, my friends, is not an opportunity we should let pass by!

KEY POINTS:

1. God allows painful situations in the lives of his followers; these can bring us great gain in the end.
2. If something happens in your life over which you have no control, you can be sure that it is God's will for you.
3. Sometimes the Lord causes things to happen in our lives, and other times he simply allows them to happen.
4. Even when we have no control over an event in our life, we still have the choice to accept it or reject it.
5. When we accept God's will during times of suffering, we are expressing our love for him in a great way.

REFLECTION QUESTIONS:

1. How do you generally react when things don't go your way?
2. Sometimes the Lord allows painful events to occur in our lives because they will help us spiritually. How do you think he feels when you complain about them?
3. Do you regularly ask Jesus to help you carry the crosses in your life?
4. Are you able to trust God even when you don't understand something that is happening in your life?
5. Are you currently suffering in any way? Are you willing to tell God that you'll accept that suffering for as long as he desires? If not, are you willing to ask him for the grace to make that statement?

CHAPTER THIRTEEN

I Need Help Now!

THROUGHOUT THIS BOOK, I HAVE PRESENTED STEPS THAT WILL HELP you discover the Lord's will for your life. I have stressed the fact that sometimes it takes a while for God to reveal his will to us. As I discussed in chapter eight, he has good reasons for taking his time. While that's all well and good, what happens when you have to make a decision in a hurry?

We all face decisions that have to be made quickly, that can't be put off for months, weeks, or even days. In this chapter, we'll look at some general rules for handling time-sensitive decisions and explore ways to avoid the stress that may accompany them. God is aware that these situations exist, and he doesn't want you to feel pressured or anxious. He will be with you every bit as much as he is when you have ample time to decide.

DON'T RUSH

While this might not sound like advice that belongs in this chapter, it's something that needs to be said: If at all possible, try not to rush when making a major decision. Only a small percentage of important decisions have to be made instantaneously.

Take a job offer, for example. Although you may be nervous about asking for additional time, most employers are more than willing to give you at least twenty-four hours to reach a decision. While an extra day may not seem like a great deal, it is more than enough time for the Lord to give you his approval.

In general, try to put off making spur-of-the-moment decisions whenever possible. Sometimes a fixed-in-stone deadline is enough to tell you not to accept the opportunity.

Commonsense Reminders

Many important decisions can be made relatively quickly if we use our God-given intellect and common sense. If you have small children at home and your boss offers you an opportunity that involves extensive travel, there's a good chance that it's not the job for you. Your state in life should be an important factor in making decisions. Being a parent is a great honor. It is a wonderful way of serving God and shouldn't be taken lightly.

Once I understood that studying for the permanent diaconate would take me away from my wife and young children for several hours each week, I knew it wasn't God's will for me. I have also learned that I can't say yes every time I'm asked to volunteer at my parish. When these opportunities conflict with my family and career responsibilities, I simply have to decline.

One of the most difficult split-second decisions we're forced to make is whether to speak up or remain silent. Suppose you're at work, sitting around the lunch table with several of your fellow employees, and one of them shares some exciting news: She has decided to move in with her boyfriend. You know that this is morally wrong, but you don't know what to do. Should you say something, or should you remain silent?

Since this situation would endanger your friend's salvation, you should seriously consider addressing it. Such an action covers two of the spiritual works of mercy: instructing the ignorant and admonishing the sinner. However, common sense dictates that this matter be discussed in private and not at the lunch table with other people present.

On the other hand, if a general moral issue is raised (such as thoughts on abortion or same sex relationships), a lunch table discussion might be beneficial. That's assuming the conversation doesn't single out a particular individual in the workplace.

The use of common sense allows us to make many spontaneous decisions with ease, as it quickly takes many options off the table. While it shouldn't be our only technique, it's a great place to start. The Lord works frequently in the natural as well as the supernatural, and the intellect is a great gift from him.

LISTEN TO THE CHURCH

Going back to chapter four, when faced with any decision, one of the best questions you should ask yourself is, "What does the Church teach?" This question holds good for decisions that need to be made quickly. When asked with a sincere heart, it might rule out many potential choices. I can say absolutely, the Lord will never ask you to do something that violates a teaching of his Church. And you can take that to the bank!

In my younger days, I'm ashamed to say, I violated this principle many times. I often ignored the teachings of the Church when they seemed too burdensome. That was a mistake.

When we're asked to lend somebody money for an abortion or vasectomy, when we're asked to be the designated driver for a night out at a "gentlemen's club," when we have to decide whether to have another beer even though we're starting to feel woozy, the answer always must be no. Why? Because the Church teaches that these things are wrong.

On the other hand, when we're tired on Sunday morning and wonder if we should go to Mass, if we're unsure about declaring our under-the-table earnings on our income taxes, if we question the need to go to confession after committing a serious sin, the answer should be yes. The Church affirms these decisions as God's will.

Let's not fool ourselves. Church teachings apply to all Catholics. They bring us closer to God and his heaven.

Ask for Help

One of the biggest mistakes we make when trying to decide something in a hurry is forgetting to ask for help. Thinking that time is of the essence, we forgo this crucial step and try to make the decision as if we were alone on an island. While it's not always possible when making a time-sensitive decision, we should at least try to get a second opinion from a trusted advisor. Doing so can prove to be a great blessing.

Even if we have to make a choice very quickly, there is often time to make a phone call or send an e-mail. The advice of a spiritual director or trusted friend can be invaluable. In times of crisis, others often see things more objectively than we do.

Sometimes our decisions must be made so quickly that we don't even have time to make a cell phone call. Rather than ignoring the "ask for help" rule, I urge you to remember to ask the someone who is always available for consultation. That "someone" is Jesus! No matter where you may find yourself or how quickly you must make a decision, you can always count on the Lord.

Even if you're in the middle of a discussion, you can mentally turn to the Lord and ask for his guidance. He understands what you are facing, including the timetable. A simple "Lord, let me know what to do" will often be enough to give you the answer you need.

Another person who's always available is Jesus's mother. Remember, she's your mother too! Ask for her intercession.

Trust God

Sometimes we're too hard on ourselves. We've made up our minds to follow the Lord's will, but we begin to panic. We worry that our actions won't be pleasing to God.

This fear is especially noticeable when we lack clear direction. That lack of clarity can cause us to freeze and do nothing. When a choice needs to be made in a hurry, the lack of clear direction can lead to anxiety.

While it is possible that all of the above steps (common sense, Church teaching, asking for help) may not provide you with a clear answer, there is a silver lining to this cloud. If the Lord remains silent and you have to make a decision in a hurry, you can safely assume that he wants you to choose the option that you think is best. Therefore, you can feel free to use your judgment to make the decision, knowing that you are pleasing him.

God wants us to trust him. That often involves walking in mystery. It also requires us to recognize the fact that God can always bring good out of evil.

> We know that in everything God works for good with those who love him, who are called according to his purpose. For those whom he foreknew he also predestined to be conformed to the image of his Son, in order that he might be the first-born among many brethren. And those whom he predestined he also called; and those whom he called he also justified; and those whom he justified he also glorified. (Romans 8:28–30)

God proved this numerous times throughout salvation history. The Bible is filled with stories of bad, even evil, decisions, but somehow God's will prevailed, and we ended up with a Savior.

If a decision has to be made quickly and we choose the option that we think will please God the most, he will be pleased. We can make this decision in confidence, knowing that he can always bring good from any option we choose. On the other hand, if we refuse to make a decision unless we receive a clear sign from heaven, how much do we really trust God?

The Most Important Decision

Jesus sometimes asked for split-second decisions. We can gain insight from the responses of some of his potential followers.

> As they were going along the road, a man said to him, "I will follow you wherever you go." And Jesus said to him, "Foxes have holes, and birds of the air have nests; but the Son of man has nowhere to lay his head." To another he said, "Follow me." But he said, "Lord, let me first go and bury my father." But he said to him, "Leave the dead to bury their own dead; but as for you, go and proclaim the kingdom of God." Another said, "I will follow you, Lord; but let me first say farewell to those at my home." Jesus said to him, "No one who puts his hand to the plow and looks back is fit for the kingdom of God." (Luke 9:57–62)

Three individuals in this passage had to make important decisions. Each expressed a desire to follow Christ, which is good. The first man was informed that it would involve sacrifice; we don't know how he responded. The other two were willing, provided that Jesus agreed to certain conditions. In what could easily be called a challenging response, the Lord instructed them that the decision to follow him had to be an unconditional one, and it had to be made at that moment!

As this book draws to a close, it's fitting that we examine the most important decision that we will ever make. It's one decision that must be made immediately; it can't be put off until tomorrow: Are you willing to seek the Lord's will above all else?

While it may seem intimidating to make the most important decision of your life right away, there really is only one clear answer: yes! If your answer is not yes, all of the information in this book will not help you. In order for you to be truly able to know God's plan for your life, you must decide that what he wants is more important than what you want.

I urge you to make the decision to follow the Lord and to make it today. It will bring you not only peace in this life but eternal happiness in the life to come. While you're certainly free to use your own words, you can also choose to repeat the following prayer, composed under the inspiration of the Holy Spirit.

> I delight to do thy will, O my God;
> thy law is within my heart. (Psalm 40:8)

Key Points

1. If at all possible, don't make important decisions too quickly.
2. When you must make a decision quickly, allow yourself to be guided by common sense, the teaching of the Church, the advice of trusted friends, and prayer.
3. If God is not giving you a clear course of action, it's often because he wants you to trust him.
4. The Lord can bring good out of any decision you make, even if it's a bad one.
5. In order to truly discover God's will, you must decide that what he wants is more important than what you want.

Reflection Questions

1. In your desire to do God's will, have you ever gone against what common sense was telling you? How did it work out?

2. How important to you are the teachings of the Catholic Church? Are all of your decisions guided by her teachings?

3. Do you have a trusted friend or spiritual director to whom you can turn for advice? Looking over your past decisions, has this person been able to see things that you didn't see?

4. Did you ever have to make a quick decision? How did you handle it? Did you ask for God's help?

5. Are you able to commit to pursuing God's will above all else? Why? Why not? What frightens you about answering yes?

Conclusion

I SINCERELY HOPE THAT THE ADVICE I'VE SHARED IN THESE PAGES proves as helpful for you as it has been for me. While the effectiveness of the material ultimately depends upon how serious you are about seeking God's will, I am confident of one thing: The Lord is very pleased with you!

How can I be sure? The mere fact that you took the time to read a book on finding God's will indicates that you have a desire to please him. That fact alone will please him very much. While many people go through life seeking pleasure and comfort, you are on a quest to discover what you can do to please God. Well done!

Seeking God's will is not something that's done once or twice in a lifetime. Rather, it should be an everyday goal. While it's true that some decisions (such as choosing a marriage partner or deciding to enter the religious life) are ideally one-time decisions, seeking and responding to the Lord's voice is something we have the opportunity to do every day.

When I speak at parishes, I often ask the audience to check their pulse and see if they're alive. After the laughter stops, I remind them to be thankful that they're not in hell. As extreme as that statement sounds, it's absolutely true. If you are alive and breathing, you still have the chance to make it to heaven, and that is something to be thankful for. Better yet, you can take comfort in the fact that the Lord wants you to end up there and is more than willing to provide you with the grace that you need.

"God our Savior…desires all men to be saved and to come to the knowledge of the truth." (1 Timothy 2: 3–4)

"The Lord is not slow about his promise as some count slowness, but is forbearing toward you, not wishing that any should perish, but that all should reach repentance." (2 Peter 3:9)

If you're able to read this, you are obviously still alive. Therefore, God has work for you to do. This statement applies equally to the young, old, healthy, and sick. As long as we're on this earth, there are tasks that he wants us to complete. Performing these tasks, whatever they may be, is the way we follow God's plan for our lives.

Some people accomplish this work in a physical manner, while others do the Lord's work through prayer. Although our tasks may be different, we all have the same basic goal in life: "Whatever you do, do all to the glory of God" (1 Corinthians 10:31). "Whatever your task, work heartily, as serving the Lord and not men, knowing that from the Lord you will receive the inheritance as your reward" (Colossians 3:23–24).

One of the most common complaints I hear is, "I feel that God is calling me to do something else with my life, but I'm not sure what it is." Having gone through this experience for several years, I understand how painful it can be. Even though you feel that the Lord wants you to do *something* else, the fact that you don't know what that *something* is usually indicates that it's not time for you to move on just yet.

On the other hand, if you do have an idea of what God wants you to do, but your plan doesn't provide you with a way of supporting yourself or your family, it's also likely that he wants you to stay put for the time being. God desires obedience more than sacrifice (see 1 Samuel 15:22; Mark 12:33), and he sometimes asks to us to serve him where we are until he gives us our next assignment. If we're not careful, our desire to serve him can transform into a desire to serve ourselves.

Accepting the uncontrollable events in life is a great way of following God's will. If you find yourself in this situation, continue to pray for guidance while embracing your duties according to your state in life. Even though Jesus is the Lord and Savior of the universe, there was a time when doing his Father's will consisted of living in Nazareth and being obedient to Mary and Joseph (see Luke 2:51).

Don't worry so much about displeasing God that you're afraid to do anything. If you seek his will, he will guide you. If he wants you to do something, he will let you know. Also, don't forget that the choices we make are not final. Sometimes an apparent failure is part of God's plan. If something doesn't work out, he may be calling you to try something else.

If you feel that the Lord is asking you to do something, don't ignore the feeling! Use the techniques presented in this book to put it to the test. If you still feel that it's God's will, take action. The Lord will let you know if you made the wrong choice or if he wants you to do something else. More importantly, he'll be very happy that you tried to do what you thought would please him.

Would you like a foolproof way for discovering God's will for your life? Believe it or not, there is something you can do to make this a reality. All you have to do is take a look at what happened to you yesterday. While God didn't necessarily cause everything to happen (especially evil), he did allow it all to happen. Nothing that occurs in your life takes place without the Lord's approval. That's an amazing concept, isn't it?

Look back over your life and see how God made his will known to you. While this can't predict the future, it can help you in the present moment. Everything that happens to you today is God's will and, ultimately, is designed to help you get to heaven. Your job is to embrace his will by accepting everything that happens and making choices that please him.

What can you do to ensure that you are following God's plan for your life? The best thing to do is pray every day for an increased desire to follow his will. "Lo, I have come to do thy will, O God" (Hebrews 10:7; see Psalm 40:7–8) is a great way to start your day!

Ultimately, God's will for us isn't complicated. He wants us to live with him forever in heaven. "We who first hoped in Christ have been destined and appointed to live for the praise of his glory" (Ephesians 1:12).

How do we get to heaven? By doing "the will of my Father who is in heaven" (Matthew 7:21)! If we strive every day to live out the "thy will be done" that we pray in the Lord's Prayer, we will arrive at our heavenly inheritance, fully clothed in the garments of salvation.

God has a plan for us. He wants us to know that plan. Continue to ask for the wisdom to do just that, and he will show you the way.

> With thee is wisdom, who knows thy works
> and was present when thou didst make the world,
> and who understands what is pleasing in thy sight
> and what is right according to thy commandments.
> Send her forth from the holy heavens,
> and from the throne of thy glory send her,
> that she may be with me and toil,
> and that I may learn what is pleasing to thee. (Wisdom 9:9–10)

NOTES

1. John Henry Newman, *Prayers, Verses, and Devotions* (San Francisco: Ignatius, 2000), p. 338.
2. *Dei Verbum*, 21.
3. There are many translations of *The Spiritual Exercises of St. Ignatius of Loyola* available online and at your local Catholic bookstore.
4. *The Spiritual Exercises*, 104.
5. *The Spiritual Exercises*, 179.
6. *The Spiritual Exercises*, 5, 23, 170.
7. *The Spiritual Exercises*, 175–188.
8. *Autograph Directories of Saint Ignatius of Loyola*, no. 18.
9. *Spiritual Exercises*, 23.
10. Lawrence J. Gesy, *The Hem of His Garment: True Stories of Healing* (Huntington, Ind.: Our Sunday Visitor, 1996), p. 63.
11. St. Alphonsus Liguori, *Uniformity With God's Will* (Rockford, Ill.: Tan, 2009), p. 9.

About the Author

Gary Zimak is a full-time Catholic evangelist and author. A frequent speaker at parishes and conferences, he is widely known for his talks on overcoming anxiety. Gary hosts a daily radio show on BlogTalkRadio and is a regular guest on *Catholic Answers Live*, EWTN's *Son Rise Morning Show*, and *Catholic Connection* with Teresa Tomeo.